Modern Language Association of America

Approaches to Teaching
World Literature

Joseph Gibaldi, Series Editor

1. Joseph Gibaldi, ed. *Approaches to Teaching Chaucer's* Canterbury Tales. 1980.
2. Carole Slade, ed. *Approaches to Teaching Dante's* Divine Comedy. 1982.
3. Richard Bjornson, ed. *Approaches to Teaching Cervantes'* Don Quixote. 1984.
4. Jess B. Bessinger, Jr., and Robert F. Yeager, eds. *Approaches to Teaching* Beowulf. 1984.
5. Richard J. Dunn, ed. *Approaches to Teaching Dickens'* David Copperfield. 1984.
6. Steven G. Kellman, ed. *Approaches to Teaching Camus's* The Plague. 1985.
7. Yvonne Shafer, ed. *Approaches to Teaching Ibsen's* A Doll House. 1985.
8. Martin Bickman, ed. *Approaches to Teaching Melville's* Moby-Dick. 1985.
9. Miriam Youngerman Miller and Jane Chance, eds. *Approaches to Teaching* Sir Gawain and the Green Knight. 1986.
10. Galbraith M. Crump, ed. *Approaches to Teaching Milton's* Paradise Lost. 1986.
11. Spencer Hall, with Jonathan Ramsey, eds. *Approaches to Teaching Wordsworth's Poetry.* 1986.
12. Robert H. Ray, ed. *Approaches to Teaching Shakespeare's* King Lear. 1986.
13. Kostas Myrsiades, ed. *Approaches to Teaching Homer's* Iliad *and* Odyssey. 1987.
14. Douglas J. McMillan, ed. *Approaches to Teaching Goethe's* Faust. 1987.
15. Renée Waldinger, ed. *Approaches to Teaching Voltaire's* Candide. 1987.
16. Bernard Koloski, ed. *Approaches to Teaching Chopin's* The Awakening. 1988.
17. Kenneth M. Roemer, ed. *Approaches to Teaching Momaday's* The Way to Rainy Mountain. 1988.
18. Edward J. Rielly, ed. *Approaches to Teaching Swift's* Gulliver's Travels. 1988.
19. Jewel Spears Brooker, ed. *Approaches to Teaching Eliot's Poetry and Plays.* 1988.
20. Melvyn New, ed. *Approaches to Teaching Sterne's* Tristram Shandy. 1989.
21. Robert F. Gleckner and Mark L. Greenberg, eds. *Approaches to Teaching Blake's* Songs of Innocence and of Experience. 1989.
22. Susan J. Rosowski, ed. *Approaches to Teaching Cather's* My Ántonia. 1989.
23. Carey Kaplan and Ellen Cronan Rose, eds. *Approaches to Teaching Lessing's* The Golden Notebook. 1989.
24. Susan Resneck Parr and Pancho Savery, eds. *Approaches to Teaching Ellison's* Invisible Man. 1989.
25. Barry N. Olshen and Yael S. Feldman, eds. *Approaches to Teaching the Hebrew Bible as Literature in Translation.* 1989.
26. Robin Riley Fast and Christine Mack Gordon, eds. *Approaches to Teaching Dickinson's Poetry.* 1989.
27. Spencer Hall, ed. *Approaches to Teaching Shelley's Poetry.* 1990.
28. Sidney Gottlieb, ed. *Approaches to Teaching the Metaphysical Poets.* 1990.

Approaches to
Teaching García Márquez's
One Hundred Years
of Solitude

Edited by
María Elena de Valdés
and
Mario J. Valdés

The Modern Language Association of America
New York   1990

Copyright © 1990 by The Modern Language Association of America

Library of Congress Cataloging-in-Publication Data

Approaches to teaching García Márquez's One hundred years of solitude
/ edited by María Elena de Valdés and Mario J. Valdés.
    p.   cm.—(Approaches to teaching world literature ; 31)
    Includes bibliographical references and index.
    ISBN 0-87352-535-3 (C) / ISBN 0-87352-536-1 (P)
    1. García Márquez, Gabriel, 1928–   Cien años de soledad.
    2. García Márquez, Gabriel, 1928–   —Study and teaching.
    I. Valdés, María Elena de.   II. Valdés, Mario J.   III. Series.
    PQ8180.17.A73C527   1990
    863—dc20   90-6555

Cover illustration for the paperback edition: Henri Rousseau, *La charmeure de
serpents*, Louvre, Paris, 1907. Photograph: Giraudon/Art Resource.

Published by The Modern Language Association of America
10 Astor Place, New York, New York 10003-6981

CONTENTS

PREFACE TO THE SERIES

In *The Art of Teaching* Gilbert Highet wrote, "Bad teaching wastes a great deal of effort, and spoils many lives which might have been full of energy and happiness." All too many teachers have failed in their work, Highet argued, simply "because they have not thought about it." We hope that the Approaches to Teaching World Literature series, sponsored by the Modern Language Association's Publications Committee, will not only improve the craft—as well as the art—of teaching but also encourage serious and continuing discussion of the aims and methods of teaching literature.

The principal objective of the series is to collect within each volume different points of view on teaching a specific literary work, a literary tradition, or a writer widely taught at the undergraduate level. The preparation of each volume begins with a wide-ranging survey of instructors, thus enabling us to include in the volume the philosophies and approaches, thoughts and methods of scores of experienced teachers. The result is a sourcebook of material, information, and ideas on teaching the subject of the volume to undergraduates.

The series is intended to serve nonspecialists as well as specialists, inexperienced as well as experienced teachers, graduate students who wish to learn effective ways of teaching as well as senior professors who wish to compare their own approaches with the approaches of colleagues in other schools. Of course, no volume in the series can ever substitute for erudition, intelligence, creativity, and sensitivity in teaching. We hope merely that each book will point readers in useful directions; at most each will offer only a first step in the long journey to successful teaching.

Joseph Gibaldi
Series Editor

PREFACE TO THE VOLUME

The project that culminated in this book began with the suggestion of the series editor, Joseph Gibaldi, that we take up the challenge of including *One Hundred Years of Solitude* in the Approaches to Teaching World Literature series. When we began the task of formulating a questionnaire and consulting the profession on the issues involved in teaching *One Hundred Years of Solitude*, a number of discoveries began to unfold. Although we had twenty-five years of experience in teaching and publishing and fifteen years of editorial experience, we were not prepared for the scope and the diversity of professional interest in this novel. Almost every day's mail brought in another viewpoint, another context, or another approach to Gabriel García Márquez's masterpiece. Our preconceived idea that the novel is taught only in Latin American literature courses and in the occasional literature-in-translation course was far off the mark. The novel is taught in Spanish and in English in a vast variety of courses and programs of study. Indeed, in our respondents' classrooms *One Hundred Years of Solitude* is often the literary work that bridges the gaps between the humanities, the social sciences, and the natural sciences.

This response reflects the novel's preeminent place in contemporary world literature. South American critics see it as a cultural document of the greatest significance. In North America some critics consider it the high point of early postmodernism. In Europe the novel has been analyzed as a revolutionary narrative steeped in the traditions of oral storytellers. *One Hundred Years of Solitude* can support these interpretations and more, because it is, above all, a magnificent story that holds readers spellbound. Its printing history in Spanish, English, French, German, Italian, and Japanese is evidence of its international appeal.

In the tradition of great storytellers from Homer to James Joyce, Franz Kafka, and Marcel Proust, García Márquez does not so much depart from or challenge the reader's sense of the real as subvert it. From a disconcerting vantage point that oversees the entire trajectory of the tale at all times, the narrator tells in twenty unnumbered chapters the story of a town in Colombia over a one-hundred-year period. The narrator constantly reminds the reader that the event being narrated is part of a plot or story and that the event will be remembered at a time still not before the reader but already inscribed in the unrepeatable chronicle of the town of Macondo.

The more one probes the makeup of this novel, the more convinced one becomes of the subtle genius with which García Márquez has replaced the standard mimetic narrative organization of the novel since the nineteenth century with a Chinese-box puzzle where a box sits within a box within a box . . . and at the smallest end of the scale is the plan for the entire series of boxes. The largest box may be the overt reference to the political and cultural history of Colombia and Latin America, as well as to the region's physical and human geography. Within this box is a chronicle, an oral history, of a town from its foundation to its demise. The town and its inhabitants, in turn, are slowly presented in a process of birth, growth, maturation, and death—in sum, the events, both commonplace and extraordinary, that were noteworthy to the townspeople within their sense of community.

Another box rests within our boxes: the history of a family from the founding couple to the last survivor. Patterns of family traits and weaknesses are demonstrated through five generations of the Buendía family. Within this family box sits yet another, the struggle of individuals to shape their own destinies—whether as philosophers, warriors, or hedonists—even though they all fail, without knowing why. The enigma of their failures leads us to the smallest of our boxes, wherein we find that the whole story we have been reading is the same manuscript that a succession of philosopher-protagonists have been trying to decode and read throughout the novel. We find that the end of the series of boxes leads us to the beginning of Latin American reality, for the truth of the quest is that solitude is both the condition and the cause of failure of social action in Latin America.

Whatever background the reader has, the novel continues to be an imaginative catalyst of historical and social reflection, as well as aesthetic fascination.

This volume, like the others in the series, has two main parts: a survey of materials used in classroom instruction and a selection of essays offering a variety of approaches to teaching the novel. Although all the correspondence we received was interesting and potentially significant for the study of the novel, our aim, in keeping with the design of the series, was fundamentally pedagogical and pragmatic: a dialogue about teaching the novel addressed to both instructors and students, whatever their specialization. The restrictions of space forced us to make difficult choices of areas, approaches, and authors. We are pleased with the results. We thank all our colleagues who took the time to write and send in completed questionnaires, especially those who proposed essays. (A list of contributors and survey respondents is included at the end of the volume.) To our collaborators we offer gratitude for their promptness in meeting deadlines and for the quality of the material they sent, and, finally, we offer our congratulations for their work.

MEV
MJV

Part One

MATERIALS

María Elena de Valdés

Editions and Translations

Gabriel García Márquez's *Cien años de soledad* was published by Editorial Sudamericana in Buenos Aires in 1967. Since that time there have been numerous printings. Another notable edition, prepared by Jacques Joset, was published in Madrid by Ediciones Cátedra in 1987. But the meticulous Joset pays homage to the care with which the first edition was prepared, adding that the only corrections made are minimal. A more recent attractive edition with excellent typeface was issued by Editorial Diana of Mexico in 1988.

The English translation, *One Hundred Years of Solitude*, was done by Gregory Rabassa for Harper and Row in 1970. The Avon paperback edition published in the United States in 1972 and the Picador paperback published in the United Kingdom in 1972 have been best-sellers with numerous printings. As with any translation of a major work of literature, in time new attempts will be made to capture the original with a different sense of English. I applaud the idiomatic achievement of Rabassa's translation of dialogue and narrative summary, but I have some dissatisfaction with his translation of the highly charged imagery and extended metaphors. Gene Dilmore gives a helpful list of translation problems in "*One Hundred Years of Solitude*: Some Translation Corrections."

The Novel and Its Author

A number of studies and commentaries focus on Gabriel García Márquez—his life, opinions, and political views—and on how the biographical data are reflected in the novel.

There is a fine line between showing that a biographical fact is relevant to the literary text and claiming that the fact has interpretive significance. The authors cited below are all careful not to cross that line. All are concerned with the stature of the author because he is the creator of *One Hundred Years of Solitude*. Especially noteworthy are the articles by the late Angel Rama. Of particular usefulness to the student is Jacques Joset's introduction, in Spanish, to his edition of the novel and the book-length introduction to the author in English by Raymond L. Williams. For other introductory works in English, see George R. McMurray's *Gabriel García Márquez* and Julio Ortega's "Latin American Literature Facing the Eighties."

Interviews with García Márquez with reference to this novel are numerous in the daily press but are somewhat limited in scope. Two that are valuable for the student are the book-length interview in Spanish with Plinio Apulayo Mendoza and C. Dreifus's interview in English. (See also Guibert.) The article by Robert L. Sims "El laboratorio periodístico de García Márquez:

Lo carnavalesco y la creación del espacio novelístico" links the author's journalistic background and the spatial structure of the novel.

Historical Background

The use of historical data in a text brimming with hyperbole and figurative language has intrigued many critics. An important example of historical examination of the novel is the book by Lucila Inés Mena, *La función de la historia en* Cien años de soledad. The issues at stake in these studies go far beyond the simple demonstration of the historical validity of the novelistic events, for the novel as myth, history, and chronicle delves into the question of reality, of appearance and illusion, of experience and dream in the modern history of Latin America.

One of the most carefully examined novelistic and historical events is the massacre of the banana workers in chapter 15. Gene H. Bell-Villada's "Banana Strike and Military Massacre: *One Hundred Years of Solitude* and What Happened in 1928," Carlos Blanco Aguinaga's "Sobre la lluvia y la historia en las ficciones de García Márquez," Lucila Inés Mena's "La huelga de la compañía bananera como expresión de lo real maravilloso americano en *Cien años de soledad*," and Robert L. Sims's "Banana Massacre in *Cien años de soledad*: A Micro-structural Example of Myth, History and Bricolage"—all examine the historical background of specific incidents in the novel—in particular, the banana massacre and the rains that all but destroy Macondo in the aftermath of the military violence.

Selma Calasans Rodríguez and Iris M. Zavala point out the link between the novel and the chronicles of exploration and conquest. The devastating civil wars known in Colombia as *la violencia*, which provide background for more than half the novel, have been studied as part of the novelistic world by Manuel Maldonado-Denis.

Helpful, too, are materials from the comprehensive study of Latin American history edited by Leslie Bethell and published by Cambridge University Press in five volumes. Although this material does not comment directly on the novel, it presents an accurate and detailed historical background for the Colombia of the novel. Especially relevant are David Bushnell's "Independence of Spanish South America"; Malcolm Deas's "Venezuela, Colombia and Ecuador: The First Half-Century of Independence" and "Colombia, 1880–1930"; William Glade's "Latin America and the International Economy, 1870–1914"; Michael M. Hall and Hobart A. Spalding's "Urban Working Class and Early Latin American Labour Movements, 1880–1930"; John Lynch's "Catholic Church in Latin America, 1830–1930"; Frank Safford's "Politics, Ideology and Society in Post-Independence Spanish America"; and Rosemary Thorp's "Latin America and the International Economy from the

First World War to the World Depression." The book by Charles W. Bergquist, *Coffee and Conflict in Colombia, 1886–1910*, is also an excellent
historical study of the crucial years of political turmoil in the novel. Generally
useful as well is Stephen Minta's *Gabriel García Márquez, Writer of
Colombia*.

Ideological Contexts

The ideological statements that abound in the novel are limited neither to
the fictional world of Macondo nor to the sphere of politics in Colombia, for
they touch on the raw nerve of insurrection—mindless and seemingly endless throughout Latin America—a response to the economic domination by
North American interests and the greed infested with brutality of Latin
American governments and their military forces.

An influential study of the novel's ideological contexts is Angel Rama's
"De Gabriel García Márquez a Plinio Apuleyo Mendoza." Interesting recent
scholarly developments include the parallels drawn along ideological lines
between African and East Indian literatures and the novel: E. V. Ramkrishnan's "Novel of Memory and the Third World Reality: Gabriel Márquez and
Chinua Achebe" and Kumkum Sangari's "Politics of the Possible."

Antonio Cornejo Polar's writing on Latin American reality is always lucid
and searching, as in "El indigenismo y las literaturas heterogéneas: Su doble
estatuto socio-cultural." Rómulo Cosse's *"Cien años de soledad*: Ideología y
plasmación narrativa"; Jesse Fernández's "La ética del trabajo y la acumulación de la riqueza en *Cien años de soledad*"; Regina Janes's "Liberals,
Conservatives, and Bananas: Colombian Politics in the Fiction of Gabriel
García Márquez"; and Alan Kennedy's "Márquez: Resistance, Rebellion and
Reading" explore the ideological development of Colombia as reflected in
the novel.

Gerald Martin's "On 'Magical' and Social Realism in García Márquez" is an
aggressively written but fine study of the ideology in the novel. José David
Saldívar's "Ideology and Deconstruction in Macondo" takes up the challenge
of the conflict between ideology and poststructuralist theory. Of related interest are Eric Mottram on existential and political controls and Lawrence M.
Porter on the political function of fantasy in García Márquez's work.

Critical Studies

Literary Contexts

A novel exists not only in a historical and a cultural context but also in a literary context—an environment of writers and writings, themes and motives, images and styles. *One Hundred Years of Solitude* invokes literary tradition with particular force. Ever since *Cien años de soledad* was first published in 1967, comparatists have been linking it with the *Amadis* and the chronicles of the New World and with García Márquez's Latin American contemporaries. Later articles developed the formal, thematic, and intertextual relations between the novel and the works of William Faulkner. Then the expansion began in earnest; critics pointed out parallels with English, French, German, Italian, Spanish, and even Afro-American literature. Noteworthy is the full-length study by Lois Parkinson Zamora, "The Apocalyptic Vision in Contemporary American Fiction: Gabriel García Márquez, Thomas Pynchon, Julio Cortázar, and John Barth." The Latin American context is examined by Roberto González Echevarría in "With Borges in Macondo"; Jorge Guzmán in "*Cien años de soledad*: En vez de dioses, el español latinoamericano"; George R. McMurray in "*The Aleph* and *One Hundred Years of Solitude*: Two Microcosmic Worlds"; and Robert G. Mead in "Aspectos del espacio y el tiempo en *La casa verde* y *Cien años de soledad*."

The comparison to Miguel de Cervantes's *Don Quixote* is by Chester S. Halka. The French literary comparison is to Marcel Proust by John P. McGowan and to Claude Simon by Robert L. Sims's "Claude Simon and Gabriel García Márquez: The Conflicts between *histoire-Histoire* and *historia-Historia*." Ute M. Saine draws out the novel's connection with Robert Musil's *Man without Qualities*. Michael Sexson examines parallels with Italo Calvino. Vera M. Kutzinski treats common points between García Márquez and Afro-American literature.

Finally, the Faulkner connection is examined by Octavio Corvalán, Nancy Lester, Elizabeth Lowe, Harley D. Oberhelman, José Luis Ramos Escobar, Susan Snell, and Lois Parkinson Zamora's second comparative study of the novel, "The End of Innocence."

Mythic Contexts

Every extended study of the novel examines myth as it is developed by García Márquez. The Hungarian scholar Katalin Kulin's *Creación mítica en la obra de García Márquez* was published in Hungarian in 1977 and in Spanish in 1980. Michael Palencia-Roth treats the archetypal and mythical dimensions of the novel in relation to the other writings of García Márquez. Lois Parkinson Zamora, as mentioned, brings out the similarities in mythic development in this novel and in Faulkner's *Absalom, Absalom!* ("End of Innocence"). Germán Darío Carrillo's "Mito bíblico y experiencia humana en *Cien años de soledad*" is one of the most extensive treatments of biblical myth in the novel. Robert L. Sims has devoted a book to the evolution of myth in García Márquez, from his early work to *One Hundred Years of Solitude*, Avril Bryan has written an essay on myth and superstition in the novel, and Stephen Hart has examined the applicability of "magical realism" to this novel.

Interpretation and Analysis

There has been an enormous production of often markedly different interpretive approaches to the novel. The differences among these approaches are found not so much in the interpretive explanations offered as in the distinctive questions asked. Such approaches have ranged from Jungian psychoanalytic commentary to Marxist allegory. Some focus on one incident; others are panoramic in scope.

Among the influential book-length studies of the novel are those by Mario Vargas Llosa, Michael Palencia-Roth, and Josefina Ludmer. Anibal González's essay offers an interesting interpretation of the novel, making use of Jacques Derrida's concepts.

In addition, Agustín Cueva's article is noteworthy for the sociological methods used. Víctor Farías's book is one of the richest philosophical studies of the novel; his premises are primarily from the Frankfurt school, and his commentary is often illuminating. Roberto González Echevarría's "*Cien años de soledad*: The Novel as Myth and Archive" is a lucid treatment of the historicity of the text. Ricardo Gullón's article has been reprinted a number of times in both Spanish and English; it is a highly readable study of the novel's narrative perspective within the Hispanic tradition. Suzanne Jill Levine's *El espejo hablado: Un estudio de* Cien años de soledad is a balanced and informed study of structure and meaning. One European scholar to take up the challenge of *One Hundred Years of Solitude* was Cesare Segre in his semiotic analysis of time in the novel. The excellent collection of interpretive essays edited by Francisco E. Porrata and Fausto Avendaño includes an article by William W. Siemens, one of the best studies of narrative structure of this novel.

The last twenty years have brought about far-reaching developments in the field of literary study through the related disciplines of textual analysis ranging from semiotic and structural studies to updated versions of discourse analysis. Among the technical studies are those by Héctor Mario Cavallari, Paul Di Virgilio, Alfonso de Toro, and Edelweis Serra. Traditional textual analysis is well represented by Noé Jitrik, Myron I. Lichtblau, and Kate Beaird Meyers. Two ground-breaking articles are Julio Ortega's "Canje,

intercambio y valor: La economía signica en *Cien años de soledad*" and
Mario Rojas's "Tipología del discurso del personaje en el texto."

Thematic studies of the novel are similarly numerous. The study of theme
invites the danger of misrepresenting the whole because of the close scrutiny
given a single thread. The selections presented here are particularly careful
studies that strive to keep the whole of the novel in sight while examining
the detail of thematic presentation.

By far the most thoroughly examined theme in the novel is that of solitude.
Among the best studies are those by Graham Burns, Sara Castro-Klaren,
Adalbert Dessau, Wendy B. Faris, David William Foster, Paul M. Hedeen,
Pablo López-Capestany, and Mary C. Pinard. All those critics examine the
narrative development of solitude, but they draw different conclusions about
its significance.

A number of critics have examined love, machismo, and incest. The article
by Gustavo Alvarez Gardeázabal is noteworthy. A general study of machismo
in García Márquez was published by Cecilia Caicedo Jurado. The theme of
incest has received more extensive treatment from critics like John Incledon
and Yolanda Osuña. The theme of alchemy in *One Hundred Years of Solitude*
has been studied by Chester S. Halka and by Kathleen McNerney and John
Martin. Time as a theme in the novel has received most attention by critics
also concerned with myth. A representative example is Lois Parkinson Zamora's "Myth of Apocalypse and Human Temporality in García Márquez's
Cien años de soledad."

Women and the Novel

A significant innovation in literary criticism in recent years has been the
unprecedented explosion of feminist criticism and theory in Europe and
North America. Although only some of the studies in this section can in any
way be called feminist, they all concentrate on the role of women in the
novel and on the mythic and political aspects of the women of Macondo.
Among the most innovative is the study by A. Sainte-Marie. A number of
studies—like those by M. Audrey Aaron, Avril Bryan, Margarita Fernández,
and Lydia D. Hazera—concentrate on single features or characters in order
to present the existential questions of being female in a macho world. Other
studies treat the sexist element as part of the narrative world: Susanne
Kappeler's "Voices of Patriarchy" and Arnold M. Penuel's "Death and the
Maiden Demythologization of Virginity."

Pedagogical Studies

Only a handful of articles consider the teaching of this novel. Susanne Kappeler's "Voices of Patriarchy" is part of a volume on teaching literature. Gene Dilmore's article on translation corrections is a practical aid to anyone teaching the novel in translation.

A useful pedagogical article is Nina M. Scott's "Inter-American Literature: An Antidote to the Arrogance of Culture," in which she describes and examines teaching the novel in a comparative mode with Faulkner. The article by Francisco E. Porrata in the book he edited with Fausto Avendaño stands out for its pedagogical efficiency and clarity in a classroom exposition of the novel's structure.

Audiovisual Materials and Related Criticism

One of the least-explored areas of García Márquez's creativity is his writing of film scripts and his use of cinematic techniques in his writing. Two studies bear directly on the subject: Matías Montes-Huidobro's "From Hitchcock to García Márquez" and M. Valencia Valderrama's "García Márquez et le cinema ou le cinema de García Márquez."

The film *Eréndira*, which García Márquez wrote, is available in video. The film is based on the author's short novel and is included in *One Hundred Years of Solitude* as a minor incident. Another video, *Gabriel García Márquez: La magia de lo real*, is an excellent introduction to the historical, geographical, and cultural background of the novel; this sixty-minute color videotape is available in both Spanish and English and contains footage of the author commenting on literature and his life.

A recording about Gabriel García Márquez is available in the British Broadcasting Corporation Twentieth-Century European Authors series, and a Mexican recording has the author reading from the novel.

Bibliographies

No bibliography is either complete or accurate. The annotated bibliography in Raymond L. Williams's Twayne volume is useful. Most extensive is Margaret Eustella Fau's 1980 bibliography, with a 1986 supplement compiled with the collaboration of Nelly Sfeir de González. It is annotated and well designed, but it lacks a number of important works listed in the annual Modern Language Association bibliography.

The bibliography by Lucila Inés Mena, "Bibliografía anotada sobre el ciclo de la violencia en la literatura colombiana," provides the scholar with a useful listing of sources for the study of the political and ideological background to the novel.

Part Two

APPROACHES

INTRODUCTION
Mario J. Valdés

Part 2 suggests a variety of academic settings, course contexts, and interpretive approaches suitable for teaching *One Hundred Years of Solitude*. The contributors have taught García Márquez's book successfully to freshman and graduate students in Canada, Mexico, and the United States; at a small, liberal arts college for women and a large technological university; at private colleges and state universities. The courses described range from lower-level interdisciplinary courses and introductions to Latin American literature for Spanish majors to a graduate comparative literature seminar focusing on theory.

An initial group of contributors were selected from the respondents to the questionnaire on the basis of how well they knew the novel and on their awareness of the pedagogical issues involved in teaching it. While it was our first contact with some of the respondents, we were pleased to find that others, already known to us through their publications on *One Hundred Years of Solitude* or their work in literary theory and criticism, similarly had a vital interest in teaching the novel.

The nature of the responses suggested the organization of part 2. It became clear that we had to address both course contexts in which the novel is taught and interpretive approaches to teaching the novel. This organization coincided with our own training and experience. María Elena de Valdés wrote her PhD thesis on curricular approaches in departments of Spanish and Latin American studies and has been involved in extensive curricular planning at various universities. For my part, most of my previous experience in the classroom and in publications has been in interpretive approaches to literature.

The different course contexts in which the novel is taught should not be measured on a scale of more or less exposure to literature but, rather, as all our contributors to this section have emphasized, should be considered as a series of different learning environments. Because the contexts clearly differ, we felt that by bringing them together in one volume, we would not only assist the teacher facing similar planning tasks but also significantly enhance the teaching of the novel in all these contexts by making manifest the richness of the novel as a source of social reflection.

The courses in which the novel is taught range widely in the six essays in the first section on curricular contexts, from courses in Latin American literature and comparative literature to humanities and women's studies courses that include science students and students in professional programs, such as law, engineering, and medicine. Yet a degree of overlap necessarily exists because the essayists address similar issues involved in teaching the novel in North American classrooms—for example, discussions of Latin American history and magical realism.

Hanna Geldrich-Leffman opens the section by recounting how students in her senior honors seminar in the humanities relate García Márquez's principles of creativity, preoccupation with language, and re-creation of history through myth to a variety of twentieth-century texts, films, and artworks through an examination of the different ways artists have of reflecting their vision of historical, social, philosophical, and artistic realities in their work. After a brief discussion of the process of comparative study, Lois Parkinson Zamora relates comparative approaches that have proved useful in courses on American identity, Caribbean contexts, time and memory, and magical realism in contemporary literature.

In courses on literature and Hispanic culture for Spanish majors, international relations majors with a specialization in Latin America, and other interested students, Chester S. Halka seeks to expose the historical and the political concerns of García Márquez by asking students to watch for connections between Macondo and the outside world through commercialization, socialization, and mechanization. María Elena de Valdés discusses a course developed for the Colegio de México's program on Latin American women, in which the students use *One Hundred Years of Solitude* to investigate how Latin American women see themselves and are seen by their community.

Sandra M. Boschetto describes her interdisciplinary course Technology in Literature, which offers her students—largely majors in the sciences and engineering—"the opportunity to explore problems pertaining to Third World development, history, politics, ideology, and ethics." Close readings and comparative analysis provoke students to reconsider what technology, machines, and waste mean to them. Because he finds that teaching literature is often secondary in the foreign language department, Walter D. Mignolo concludes the section by considering ways to bring critical thought into the classroom; through a comparison of oral and written narratives, students grow to understand what a novel is and then what a Latin American novel is.

The interpretive approaches represented in part 2 are not intended to be a survey of the different ways in which the novel can be examined most profitably; there are, of course, many effective approaches. But the six essays in this section have all been written with the teacher-student relationship in mind, and they emphasize the teacher's preparation of the text for classroom presentation.

To begin this section, Gabriela Mora situates her reading of *One Hundred Years of Solitude* in its historical context in order to uncover the ideological values woven in and to bring "students closer to the total message of the book." The objective of Isabel Alvarez Borland's approach is to uncover the interaction between the text's historical, mythical, and metafictive aspects. Robert L. Sims analyzes the subtextual level of *One Hundred Years of Solitude* by using archetypal criticism, a method he finds useful for literature in translation courses that encompass a wide variety of topics. Gary Eddy applies analytical psychology to the novel, focusing on the Buendía family as "doomed because it is forever unable to integrate the everpresent contents and images of the unconscious into its waking life." Next, I use a phenomenological approach to bring the disciplinary lines between history and literature together as complementary partners. By probing the meaning of and the response to telling historical and fictive events, students can develop a personal sense of the text that can be shared with others. In the final essay, Amaryll Chanady uses *One Hundred Years of Solitude* to introduce the methods of narratology to graduate students.

Page references in the essays refer to the Avon English-language edition of *One Hundred Years of Solitude*. When two numbers appear in parentheses, the first refers to the Sudamericana Spanish-language edition.

We are pleased with the results of the project. All contributors have written richly rewarding essays on the curricular contexts and interpretive approaches to teaching *One Hundred Years of Solitude*. The roundtable is open for the wider participation of our readers.

COURSE CONTEXTS

One Hundred Years of Solitude
in Humanities Courses

Hanna Geldrich-Leffman

My aim in the honors senior seminar Visions of Reality is to present to the students—within the context of the historical, social, philosophical and artistic realities of the twentieth century—the ways that artists have been seeing those realities and reflecting their visions in their works. The honors program has always required intermediate-level competence in a foreign language, and that requirement has been extended to all students since the fall of 1987. I use a comparative approach because students come from different majors and have different linguistic backgrounds. I also think that such an approach liberates students from the almost exclusive hold of English-speaking authors and opens up new vistas. This aim has been appreciated and well accepted by the students.

The syllabus for the seminar consists of the following works: Franz Kafka, *The Trial*; Jorge Luis Borges, *Ficciones*; Jean-Paul Sartre, *No Exit* and *The Flies*; Eugène Ionesco, *Rhinoceros*; Juan Rulfo, *The Burning Plain*; Gabriel García Márquez, *One Hundred Years of Solitude*; Paul Celan, "Poems"; and Christa Wolf, *Cassandra*. Except for Ionesco, Rulfo, and Celan, each author is allotted two class periods. Besides the literary works, I incorporate several films into the course for viewing by the students on their own time. Some are film versions of works discussed (for example *The Trial*, by Orson Welles); others are models or examples of a particular literary style (Charlie Chaplin's *Modern Times*); still others are movie versions of works not discussed in class (*The Lost Honor of Katherina Blum* by Volker Schlöndorff and Margarethe von Trotta). Thus, the vision of the author is viewed as though through a double exposure. By using these movies, I broaden the points of view, exemplify the possibilities of the different media—words versus images—and show the enrichment to be gained by cross-fertilizing the visual and the verbal arts.

To introduce the students to the theme of the course, visions of reality, I bring in slides of paintings and photographs that represent different styles and ways of representing reality. We concentrate on two motifs: portraits of women and landscapes, since they concretize how manifold the ways of seeing, of representing, and of creating are. From Jan Vermeer to Pablo Picasso, from the photograph of a young girl to an American landscape, technique, composition, point of view, color, and the play of light and shadow are conditioned by the need of the artist to transform the reality seen into a new artistic vision. This leads into a discussion of the terms *reality* and *vision* and of the differences and parallels between seeing and saying—that is, between visual and verbal expressions. The discussion often turns to the difficulty of expressing meaning through language, of revealing or hiding reality or truth through words. At this point we usually examine different forms of language—like commercials, propaganda slogans, and a poem—to show how artists can transform reality according to their needs or desires.

One Hundred Years of Solitude comes in the second half of the course, after the students have grappled with the labyrinthian world of Kafka, the intellectual constructs of Borges, existentialism, the absurd, and the seemingly hopeless world of Rulfo. (I follow a loosely chronological order to help the students gain a historical perspective in the development of ideas and stylistic trends.) The text used is the Gregory Rabassa translation, but the Spanish version is put on reserve in the library, and the students who have studied Spanish are encouraged to read as much as possible in the original. Since this is a senior honors course, I never check whether or not they do it, but through conversations, occasional papers that use Spanish bibliographies, and casual references, I know that most of the students see this invitation as a challenge and are eager to prove to themselves that they can do it; consequently they do read at least part of the work in the original.

Before we start discussing García Márquez's novel, the students look up the terms *magical realism, myth,* and *baroque* and are assigned specific chapters on which the discussion will center. The students are responsible for acquiring biographical and general stylistic data. For oral presentations I usually suggest topics that deal with historical, philosophical, or artistic matters. A discussion of García Márquez usually involves a presentation on the Latin American situation or a more specific discussion of Colombia, the economic involvement of the United States in the "banana republic," or the personal background of the author himself. This is an important part of the course, not because our analysis of the works is historical or biographical but because many of the students lack the necessary background knowledge to appreciate the works. To give an added visual dimension, I show excerpts of the video *Gabriel García Márquez: La magia de lo real* to the class, since it gives them a feeling for the reality of García Márquez's world.

Our class discussions revolve around three general topics: (1) magical realism: what it is, how it is expressed in this work, why the author uses this style, and what he accomplished with it; (2) myth: in general, what it is, what kind of myths the author uses in this work, and why; and (3) the creation of the work of art: the use of language, involvement of the reader, and what new vision was achieved. To tie the García Márquez novel to the other works in the course, we look at what this particular vision of reality has contributed to our own appreciation of reality.

To help the students in their analysis, I suggest several secondary sources as background reading (Carrillo, Earle, Giacoman, McGuirk and Cardwell, Maturo, Shaw and Vera-Godwin), especially Mario Vargas Llosa's critique of García Márquez for those who can read Spanish; in class I point to the latter as an example of what insights one Latin American author can bring to the work of another. The discussion of magical realism starts easily either after the viewing of *La magia de lo real* or during our textual analysis of the first section of the novel and José Arcadio's encounter with ice. The students are asked to define *the real*, *realism*, and *magic*; physical or historic reality; and creative, spiritual, and symbolic reality. We examine the shock of the first encounter with the unknown reality of ice and the imbuing of this reality with a magical, psychic reality that surfaces throughout the novel in dreams and images of mirrors, reflecting the creative energies generated by the encounter. As other examples of magical realism emerge, the discussions deal with the historical realities of Colombian politics, the fights between Liberals and Conservatives, the coming of the Americans, the prevalent social structures, machismo, the role of women, the presence of the Catholic church, and the "reality," for instance, of Remedios the Beauty's assumption into the heavens while hanging out sheets. The students see how the author transforms the simple reality of a Colombian small town and the historical, social reality of Latin America into a creative realm that transcends the limits of time and space, just as the character of Melquíades is seen as the priest-magician, the author of the manuscripts, presiding over this magical creation.

The magical element leads into the next phase of our analysis, the mythic dimension. I define myth as a language, as a story of origins, and as the creative process of self-definition. García Márquez uses myths from the classical, the Judeo-Christian, and the Indian traditions and at the same time creates his own. I start the discussion with myths of foundation. Not only does the magical, supernatural element appear immediately in the form of divine intervention or taboo, but so also do the initial pairings of two brothers (or two males in conjunction with a female), the elements of transgression and violence, and the consequent expulsion and moving to a new foundation. The transgression of a taboo (jumping over the wall in the case of Romulus

and Remus, eating from the tree in the case of Adam and Eve, incest in
One Hundred Years) and the consequent violence (the killing of Remus and
the initial killing in the war of Troy, the killing of Abel by Cain, the killing
of Prudencio Aguilar by José Arcadio Buendía) reveal patterns that tie the
narratives into a common mythic tradition of the foundation of a new society.
It also leads to analysis of the mythic symbolism of trees and water and to
speculations about the symbolic function of such names as Macondo, Ursula,
José, Arcadio, Melquíades. Reference to the Oedipus myth brings into
awareness the mythical search for identity and self-definition in the novel.
The students are already aware of the importance of this element in contemporary Latin American writing from our previous discussion of Juan
Rulfo's work. I bring in excerpts from Octavio Paz to illustrate the point and
to make the students conscious of the cultural differences noted by the
Mexican critic. Just as Aureliano Babilonia finally deciphers the manuscripts
and discovers his own identity, history, and fate, the students grapple with
the reader's role in the creation of the text and can discuss language and
the creation of the new reality, the work of art.

Since the seminar is composed of some of the best and brightest students
at Loyola College, classroom discussions are lively and generate stimulating
exchanges of ideas. At this point loose strands of the discussions usually start
to come together, and the students notice the underlying structure of *One
Hundred Years*. We look at the text from the point of view of its language,
structure, and composition; we notice the apparent discrepancies between
Melquíades the author of the manuscripts and Melquíades the character in
the novel and between Aureliano Babilonia the reader of the manuscripts
and Aureliano Babilonia the character in the manuscripts. A student may
note an apparent parallel between the author-narrator Melquíades and author García Márquez on the one hand and the reader and Aureliano Babilonia
on the other hand. Reader-response theory helps clarify reader participation
in the creation of the text; the image of the speaking mirror suddenly makes
sense. The students see the possible identification of the reader with the
last member of the Buendía family, who is deciphering the text just as they
have been doing, making the students part of the inner magic circle of the
textual web. Stylistic peculiarities are noted, such as the baroque character
of the novel, with its gargantuan exaggerations, profusion of details, gro-
tesque humor, and earthy descriptions of sexual exploits intermingled with
poetic images of butterflies, showers of yellow flowers, and magic occur-
rences. The students become aware of the parallel between the boundless
energy embodied in sexuality as the creative principle and the energy in
the creation of the work of art; the two acts of creation operate on different
levels but are united by the outcome of vitality and new life. Incest is noted
to be the fear of sterility and the creation of monsters, harking back to
primeval chaos rather than to the quest for a more spiritual, higher life form.
As we pull everything together from our discussions, the students note how

the reality of García Márquez's world, the microcosm within the macrocosm of the reality of Colombia and Latin America, becomes transformed through his vision and creative art into the new reality and myth of *One Hundred Years of Solitude*.

What remains is to make connections with the other literary works discussed—to show similar principles of creativity, similar preoccupations with language, and the re-creation of history through myth. For instance, we note parallels with Celan's poetry and the transformation through language of the horror of the holocaust; with Christa Wolf's new reading of the myth of the Trojan War and the story of Cassandra; with the power of language, even in its misuse, in yellow journalism in the filmed version of Heinrich Böll's *Lost Honor of Katherina Blum*; with the breakdown of logic and language in Ionesco's *Rhinoceros*; with the magical reflection of landscape in the inner world of Rulfo's characters. We also note the creation of a new reality through language, especially in the stories of Borges and the metaphor of Kafka's *Trial*. Finally, the mastery and the unique peculiarities of García Márquez become apparent, and the students see the reasons for his inclusion in this course—his Latin American vision and that unique blend of the real and the magical that puts him close to fairy tales and myths; they see him as the creator of a new vision of reality.

One Hundred Years of Solitude in Comparative Literature Courses

Lois Parkinson Zamora

Gabriel García Márquez's *One Hundred Years of Solitude* is a richly suggestive novel that is read and taught in conjunction with literary texts from all
over the world. To state that the novel lends itself to comparative literary
study is, then, to state the obvious. But the popularity of the work may
make definition and a discussion of comparative approaches desirable. My
aim here is to define comparative literary study generally and to propose
four comparative contexts and groups of texts in which García Márquez's
novel may be examined and understood. Because comparative conclusions
about any literary text depend on the texts with which it is compared, my
initial generalizations would be useless without the specific comparative
contexts and textual groupings that I propose in the second part of my essay.

Literary comparatists are concerned with the relations of literary texts
across linguistic and cultural boundaries. The analytical tools and the critical
methods of the comparatist resemble those of other literary critics. The
comparatist, however, stresses the relative qualities of texts because the
comparing and the contrasting of texts uncover similarities and differences
essential to critical analysis. As the term itself suggests, comparative literary
study sets in motion a process: the comparatist looks first at one text, then
at another and another, returning to the first with an enlarged perspective
on its meaning and on the literary mechanisms that generate its meaning.
Thus, the comparative process may be both indirect and direct for any text.
The successful comparatist creates an interacting and mobile structure of
textual relations that shed light on each of the texts.

A comparative approach requires competence in more than one language
and knowledge of more than one literary tradition or culture. But, because
of the constraints of time and students' varying levels of competence in
foreign languages, it may be justifiable to teach texts in translation. When
I do so, I find that what is lost in translation is offset by the increased
sensitivity to cultural and textual differences that literary comparisons require and instill. *One Hundred Years of Solitude* has introduced countless
non-Spanish speakers to Latin American literature and has inspired them
to study other Latin American texts and traditions. Comparative literary
study in the United States should foster this enlarged perspective on our
shared American territory. Therefore, I refer to literary works by their
translated titles, even though it is preferable to read them in the original.

The grounds for the comparative study of literary texts vary enormously,
and we must be clear about the motivations for comparing particular texts
and authors. Any comparative discussion should begin by asking, Why these
texts and not others? Answers to this question emerge during the discussion,
but the comparatist's choices must be addressed early on. The issue of text
selection is thus foregrounded in comparative courses, as it is not in most

other literature courses. Whereas most literature courses study texts written in one form (poetry, fiction, drama) or during one time period in one country (modern American fiction, eighteenth-century British literature), comparative courses study texts because of their interrelations and connections to other texts. Generally, the grounds for literary comparisons are historical, cultural, and formal; interartistic studies are also increasingly common. These grounds are rarely isolated but rather overlap and inform one another.

Historically organized comparative courses often investigate broad aesthetic movements or generic developments: a style or movement, a mode or genre (the European baroque, Romanticism in England and Germany, the rise of the novel). Because the forms and values of historical movements are often expressed in various art media, interartistic comparisons are likely to be useful. Historical categories may also structure more specific comparisons: studies of a writer's sources and influences, studies of a work's or a writer's reception into another language and culture. A writer's sources are reflected in the literary text, but more than just textual resemblance is required to make assertions about influences. Here, biographical information is often useful. Does the writer state his or her influences? Did the writer read the works or the writers reflected in the literary text? Reception studies also require extratextual investigation. They ask how and when literary works move across linguistic boundaries into other literary cultures, and they often investigate the cultural and material mechanisms that condition that movement. The studies may, for example, discuss translating and publishing practices, book distribution, book reviewing, and the social and political position of writers and literature in the receiving culture.

Literary relations between or among cultural territories (whether countries or continents) is a second broad category of comparative literary study, and it overlaps the historical model. Whether a course such as Romanticism in England and Germany emphasizes cultural definition over historical definition depends on its aims. Even if a primary aim of the course is to investigate Romanticism as a historical movement, the different literary traditions and sensibilities of English and German literature during that historical period naturally condition the discussion. In short, many courses are concerned with both historical and cultural definition and share significant analytical aims and procedures. I propose here two comparative cultural territories—a hemispheric American context and a Caribbean context—in which to place *One Hundred Years*.

A third general category of comparative literary studies compares texts according to related formal characteristics, such as related themes or motifs, narrative techniques, and poetic devices. We are all familiar with courses that are organized thematically. Such courses, because they could expand almost infinitely, may require some further organizing and delimiting principle, whether chronological or geographical (the heroic quest in medieval European narrative, theology and contemporary literature). In courses organized according to the thematic relations of texts, an interartistic discussion may be useful in expanding the students' understanding of the various expressions of the theme. Comparative courses based on related narrative or poetic techniques often involve the discussion of genre as such and the development of genres over time (point of view in the self-conscious novel, the classical tradition and Renaissance lyric poetry). In this comparative category, I propose two more comparative contexts in which to place *One Hundred Years*.

I have stressed the importance of the choice of literary texts in comparative studies. Every comparative literature course creates a fluid set of textual relations; different groupings of texts result in different interactions and different insights. The substitution of a single text on a syllabus shifts the comparative relations of the rest, so it is appropriate that I list potential selections at the outset of each of the comparative contexts outlined below. I offer these sample syllabuses with the understanding that other choices could have been made and with the hope that my readers will be inspired to make their own.

My first two textual groupings are an introduction to inter-American literary relations. The texts and authors listed are basic to this comparative context. Further courses in this comparative area may include less well known novels and novelists and may narrow the comparative territory thematically, geographically, and historically. To generate a variety of ideas for pairings and groupings, I list more texts than can easily be taught in a semester university course or a year-long high school course. Indeed, a two-semester university course would be ideal for my first grouping of texts. The appropriate number of texts for a particular course varies according to the level and the abilities of the students and the desired depth and detail of discussion. I do not recommend particular critical theories or methods of reading on my sample syllabuses, though I do suggest appropriate critical studies. As I have said, comparatists use the same analytical tools as noncomparatists: depending on their aims, they find useful critical tools and angles of vision in structuralist, semiotic, Marxist, feminist, deconstructive, and other models of literary analysis. Whatever the texts and the critical theories decided on, the historical and cultural backgrounds needed to situate texts in a comparative context are likely to be greater than in a noncomparative context. Your students should be advised that their comparative undertaking will be both arduous and rewarding.

Communal Identities in the Americas (A Comparative Survey of American Literary Relations)

Ancestral Presences

The Labyrinth of Solitude, Octavio Paz (Mexico)
In the American Grain, William Carlos Williams (U.S.)

True History of the Conquest of New Spain (1568), Bernal Díaz del
    Castillo
Brief Relation of the Destruction of the Indies (1552), Bartolomé de
    las Casas
The General History of Virginia (1624), John Smith
Of Plymouth Plantation (1630), William Bradford

American Myths, American Memory

One Hundred Years of Solitude, Gabriel García Márquez (Colombia)
Absalom, Absalom! William Faulkner (U.S.)
What's Bred in the Bone, Robertson Davies (Canada)

The Frontier: Civilization and Barbarism

The Pioneers, James Fenimore Cooper (U.S.)
Doña Bárbara, Rómulo Gallegos (Venezuela)
Or *Facundo*, Domingo Faustino Sarmiento (Argentina)
Or *Deep Rivers*, José María Argüedas (Peru)

Female Archetypes and America as Eden

"Rappaccini's Daughter," Nathaniel Hawthorne (U.S.)
Aura, Carlos Fuentes (Mexico)
Or selections from *The New Islands*, María Luisa Bombal (Chile)
Or selections from *Enclosed Garden*, Angelina Muñiz-Huberman
    (Mexico)

The Usable Past

Distant Relations, Carlos Fuentes (Mexico)
The Song of the Lark, Willa Cather (U.S.)
Or *The Lost Steps*, Alejo Carpentier (Cuba)
Or *Don Segundo Sombra*, Ricardo Güiraldes (Argentina)
Or "The Bear," William Faulkner (U.S.)

Individualism and Opportunism

Adventures of a Young Man, John Dos Passos (U.S.)
The Death of Artemio Cruz, Carlos Fuentes (Mexico)

The Voices and Images of Popular Culture

Betrayed by Rita Hayworth, Manuel Puig (Argentina)
The Moviegoer, Walker Percy (U.S.)

Allegories of Power: The Political Present

*Lives on the Line: The Testimony of Contemporary Latin American
    Authors*, ed. Doris Meyer

The House of the Spirits, Isabel Allende (Chile)
House in the Country, José Donoso (Chile)

Postmodernist *Ficciones* (Selected Stories)

Jorge Luis Borges (Argentina)
Julio Cortázar (Argentina)
Felisberto Hernández (Uruguay)
Donald Barthelme (U.S.)
Robert Coover (U.S.)

The comparative American contexts suggested in this syllabus and in the one that follows have been devised with García Márquez's masterpiece at the center, but the center of what? Several issues of hemispheric politics are raised by comparative courses in American literature, issues that are not limited to literary relations. In the first place, to what extent may we use the word *American* to refer to the entire hemisphere? In the United States we have appropriated the word to describe ourselves, but other residents of the Americas are, in fact, also Americans and think of themselves as such. Teaching a comparative course in American literature makes sense only when United States students think of *America* as including Latin America, Canada, and the Caribbean. This is not a trivial point because, if the students are internationally oriented, they are likely to think in terms of an east-west (Europe–United States) axis, not a north-south one. A vision of an America that extends from pole to pole, not merely "from sea to shining sea," is basic to comparative American courses. An increased awareness of cultural and political relations in the Americas may be one of their most important effects.

Having insisted on an enlarged definition of *America*, we encounter further problems. I have proposed that we compare North American and South American texts. But is it accurate to think of either geographical area as an entity? And, if we do, are the terms not wildly asymmetrical? Of the thirty-five countries and fifteen territories or protectorates in North America and South America, only two—Canada and the United States—seem unequivocally North American. Central America and the Caribbean are in the northern hemisphere, of course, but for comparative purposes it makes more sense to link most Central American and Caribbean countries culturally to South America, rather than geographically to North America. The term *Latin American* may help us here, but to speak of Latin American literature may be misleading in its implication of an integrated geographical and literary entity. The countries of Latin America differ greatly one from another ethnically, economically, politically, and linguistically, but they also share cultural and historical features. Contemporary fiction from Latin America exhibits common features that critics and readers increasingly recognize as Latin American, whether the author is Colombian or Brazilian or Mexican. So, despite the recognized cultural diversity of Latin America, I am proposing comparative courses that assume the formulation *Latin American literature* to be a valid and useful one.

As is clear from the list of texts above, this first course proposal is organized according to comparative relations that are historical, geographical, and thematic. Though my thematic subheadings are no more than suggestive, they provide students with an additional organizational structure (beyond the historical and the geographical) to lessen the initial impression of an overly daunting and undefinable set of texts. For the same reason, I suggest that our comparative project proceed dialectically, usually by pairs, so that the students may place works side by side for comparison and contrast.

The collections of essays by Octavio Paz and William Carlos Williams listed at the beginning of this course can be used to advantage in almost any comparative American course. Both comparative studies raise the question of whether there is or can ever be a hemispheric cultural entity referred to as "America," and they look to the historical past, as well as the present, for insights and answers. Their essays are informed by an awareness of the problems of approaching "the other"—those culturally and linguistically different from the dominant ideology or from one's own ideology. (Tzvetan Todorov's *Conquest of America*, Edward Said's *Orientalism* and *Covering Islam*, Fredric Jameson's "Third-World Literature," and Aijaz Ahmad's "Jameson's Rhetoric of Otherness" may provide an additional ideological framework for this introductory discussion.) If the teacher does not wish to teach all the essays in the collections by Paz and Williams, I recommend one of Paz's essays in particular. It is entitled "Mexico and the U.S.," and it has been appended to the original group of essays in *The Labyrinth of Solitude* in its 1985 United States edition. It reminds students of the vast differences in the indigenous populations and the European patterns of colonization in the Anglo-Saxon and Hispanic Americas. These differences, as well as the shared experience of settling a New World, resonate in all the paired works that follow it in this course.

The teacher may prefer to emphasize fictional texts over nonfictional ones and hence to exclude the chronicles and the histories of the earliest European settlers that I have listed in the first section of this syllabus. In that case an initial discussion of García Márquez's *One Hundred Years of Solitude* and Faulkner's *Absalom, Absalom!* can raise many of the same questions about cultural and national identity as the first works written in the New World. These contemporary novels also explore the history and the myth of America: they look back to the origins of a specifically American community; they trace the progressive decline of that community, the land, and its individual inhabitants; they describe families who reflect the burden of historical circumstance, which both authors conceive as destiny. Both novels posit narrators who stand beyond the end of the histories they narrate and sense overwhelmingly their cultures' failures to realize the historical desires of the founding fathers. On my sample syllabus I have grouped *What's Bred in the*

Bone by the Canadian novelist Robertson Davies with *One Hundred Years* and *Absalom, Absalom!* because it is comparable in its exploration of Canadian national and cultural identity. Though it may be enough to deal with the comparative literary relations between the United States and Latin America, if you wish to add Canadian literature to the comparative discussion and the definition of American literature, Davies's novel is an appropriate and interesting way to do so.

Comparative studies have been published of *One Hundred Years* and *Absalom, Absalom!* and several of the other works on my sample syllabus (see Corvalán; Faris, "Marking Space"; McGowan; Pérez Firmat; Valdés; Zamora, *Writing the Apocalypse*). The thematic subheadings on my sample syllabus suggest some of the directions that comparative inquiry may take after the initial discussion of the two novels. Many other directions are available, but in a course designed to compare recent literary expressions of American cultural identity, I recommend *One Hundred Years* and *Absalom, Absalom!* as essential points of departure.

The Caribbean Context (Modern American Fiction)

One Hundred Years of Solitude, Gabriel García Márquez (Colombia)
Absalom, Absalom!, William Faulkner (U.S.)
The Kingdom of This World, Alejo Carpentier (Cuba)
Rulers of the Dew (Gouverneurs de la rosée), Jacques Roumain (Haiti)
Pedro Páramo, Juan Rulfo (Mexico)
Distant Relations, Carlos Fuentes (Mexico)
The Confessions of Nat Turner, William Styron (U.S.)
Beloved, Toni Morrison (U.S.)
The House of Breath, William Goyen (U.S.)
Macho Camacho's Beat, Luis Rafael Sánchez (Puerto Rico)

This grouping of texts narrows the American territory explored in my first sample syllabus and creates a comparative context to consider the New World phenomenon of *mestizaje*—cultural, racial, and literary mixing—and the ways in which writers have described and dealt with the challenges of cultural and racial pluralism. Alejo Carpentier's essay "Lo barroco y lo real maravilloso" provides an introduction to this comparative subject. My sample syllabus includes novels by Hispanic and French Caribbean writers and novels from and about the United States South.

Here again, I propose beginning with a comparative discussion of *One Hundred Years* and *Absalom, Absalom!* García Márquez himself insists on the pairing, citing the primary influence of Faulkner on his work. In his acceptance of the 1982 Nobel Prize, García Márquez calls Faulkner his "maestro," his teacher (Ortega, *Powers of Fiction*). Elsewhere he has described his affinity for Faulkner's worldview, and he redraws the map of the Caribbean to reflect that affinity. Referring to Faulkner's Mississippi, he says, "Yoknapatawpha County has Caribbean shores; thus, in some sense Faulkner is a Caribbean writer, in some sense a Latin American writer" (García Márquez and Vargas Llosa 53). The reasons for including United States Southern works in a Caribbean context go beyond García Márquez's assertion to the shared historical and cultural experiences of these regions. It is wise to begin by establishing the connections between the United States South and the more usual definition of the Caribbean region.

Carlos Fuentes has said of the literature of the United States South:

> Until recently, American writers never had the chance to deal with a national failure. The American ideal of success has done a great deal to standardize American art forms. That's why I think that for many years the most original American writing has come from the South, where there had been a real sense of regional tragedy and where there was a need to re-examine the things that had been taken for granted. ("Fuentes to Sharp" 9)

Fuentes overstates his case, of course. Other United States writers have known that one must bear the burden of the past, but that does not obviate Fuentes's point. Contemporary Latin American writers have found in the literature of the South elements akin to their own national experiences: colonial appropriation of land and culture, a decadent aristocracy, injustice and racial cruelty, belated modernization and industrial development. In *Absalom, Absalom!*, Thomas Sutpen goes to Mississippi from Haiti, where he has had an effective apprenticeship in cruelty on a Haitian sugar plantation.

Beyond these political and social parallels are similarities in religious attitudes and belief systems. Though Catholicism in Latin America and fundamentalist Protestantism in the South may initially seem more different than alike, they share essential features. The biblical tradition in the South is characterized by its literal reading of biblical images, events, and prophecies and its impulse to understand reality allegorically. The miraculous and the demonic may be just below the surface of the everyday South, and Southern history has sometimes been understood in those terms. In the biblical understanding of the irrational forces operating in history, several characters in *Absalom, Absalom!* would surely agree with Fernanda in *One Hundred Years*: "If they believe it in the Bible . . . I don't see why they shouldn't believe it from me" (277).

Once Caribbean attitudes and affinities have been suggested in this initial pairing, the students may make connections and distinctions in the novels' portrayals of cultural and national identity, narrative techniques, and specific sociopolitical concerns. These novels are cognate in the portrayal of the use and the abuse of the land and of those who work the land, the exploration of the possibility and often the failure of meaningful community, the use of multiple narrators and narrative perspectives, the creation of spiritual-magical realities in the worlds they describe. In this comparative context one may also include García Márquez's novel *Love in the Time of Cholera*, which is set in a coastal Caribbean city at the turn of the century and offers a rich portrait of the place and the time. Fuentes's *Distant Relations* considers Mexico as a part of the historical and political development of the Caribbean region, and its central section looks back to nineteenth-century Caribbean colonization and exploitation by the French and the Spanish. Other novels on my sample syllabus are less explicit in their sense of an overarching Caribbean regional identity, but they contribute to a literary definition of the region by their descriptions of countries and cultures within the region.

In Search of History: Time and Memory in Modern Narrative

> *One Hundred Years of Solitude*, Gabriel García Márquez (Colombia)
> *Swann's Way*, Marcel Proust (France)
> *Orlando* or *To the Lighthouse*, Virgina Woolf (England)
> *Manhattan Transfer*, John Dos Passos (U.S.)
> *The Magic Mountain*, Thomas Mann (Germany)
> *Journey to the End of the Night*, Louis-Ferdinand Céline (France)
> *Let Us Now Praise Famous Men*, James Agee and Walker Evans (U.S.)
> *The Life and Times of Michael K*, J. M. Coetzee (South Africa)

One of the most written-about characteristics of *One Hundred Years* is its historical perspective: its circular and linear temporal patterns, its mythic history of the New World that coexists with the specifics of Colombian history, its sweeping narrative perspective. In its concern with the thematics of history, *One Hundred Years* is part of an important current in twentieth-century fiction. The nature of time and memory and how to embody them in fictional narration are central issues in the works listed above. Comparative studies have been published on García Márquez, Proust, and Woolf, and a sizable proportion of the noncomparative critical studies of *One Hundred Years* addresses the historical patterns and events reflected in the fictional one-hundred-year history of Macondo. Melquíades's narrative situation connects the subject of history to the problem of its telling. We are witnesses to the genesis and the apocalypse of Macondo through the eyes of Melquíades, an errant gypsy who defies his own temporal limits—he comes back from the dead—to write the hundred-year history of the Buendía family in a room where, we are told, it is always March and always Monday. Other García Márquez novels are also concerned with the nature and the narration of the past; reading *The Autumn of the Patriarch* and *Chronicle of a Death Foretold* in this comparative context allows students to appreciate further the ways in which this theme pervades and structures García Márquez's art.

Because I have already emphasized the importance of the comparative link between García Márquez and Faulkner, I have not included Faulkner on this syllabus. However, *Absalom, Absalom!* or *The Sound and the Fury* or the collection of stories *Go Down, Moses* is appropriate in this comparative context. I have also excluded another major work of this century, James Joyce's *Ulysses*, because of its length and complexity. However, I also propose here the possibility of a comparative course on just four authors: Proust, Joyce, Faulkner, and García Márquez. There is great potential in the comparative investigation of the temporal modes of these monumental modernists and García Márquez. Such a concentrated comparative focus allows for a detailed discussion of relevant philosophers and philosophies of time and memory (Bergson's *durée*, Vico's spiraling stages of human history, biblical patterns of prophetic and apocalyptic narrative) and the application of critical theories of narrative temporality (Georges Poulet's historical distinctions in *Studies in Human Time*, Mikhail Bakhtin's critical formulation of the chronotope in *The Dialogic Imagination*).

Magical Realism in Contemporary Narrative

> *One Hundred Years of Solitude*, Gabriel García Márquez (Colombia)
> *The Tin Drum*, Günter Grass (Germany)
> *Midnight's Children*, Salman Rushdie (India)
> *The House of the Spirits*, Isabel Allende (Venezuela, Chile)
> *Beloved*, Toni Morrison (U.S.)
> *House in the Country*, José Donoso (Chile)
> *Aké: The Years of Childhood*, Wole Soyinka (Nigeria)
> Selections from *We Love Glenda So Much* and *A Change of Light*,
>   Julio Cortázar (Argentina)
> Selections from *Magical Realist Fiction: An Anthology*, ed. David Young
>   and Keith Hollaman

Critical studies tend to stress the *magical* in magical realism, but I emphasize the realism in this literature and orient the comparative discussion toward its political content. The nature and the narration of history is a central concern of *One Hundred Years*. This concern pervades many other contemporary Latin American novels, whose authors, like García Márquez, have often used fantastic events and characters to address the abuses of contemporary political and social institutions. A number of recent Latin American writers project expansive mythic regional histories: Mario Vargas Llosa (*The War of the End of the World*), Carlos Fuentes (*Terra Nostra*), José Donoso (*The Obscene Bird of Night* and *House in the Country*), Augusto Roa Bastos (*I the Supreme*), Alejo Carpentier (*Explosion in a Cathedral*), José Lezama Lima (*Paradiso*), Reinaldo Arenas (*The Ill-Fated Peregrinations of Fray Servando*). Any of these novels can be added to the syllabus to suggest the ways in which Latin American magical realists are erasing and redrawing the lines between fiction and history for particular political purposes. The term *magical realism* has been widely and loosely used, and a critic has dismissed it as "a conceptually poor representation of the specific differences that shape Latin American text and culture" (Ortega, *Powers of Fiction* ii). Perhaps so, but even this dismissive assessment can be tested and affirmed or refuted only in a comparative context.

This course requires an initial working definition of *magical realism* that is then revised and supplemented as the discussion progresses. A basic definition is proposed by David Young and Keith Hollaman in the introduction to their anthology *Magical Realist Fiction*, though I emphasize the need for close attention to the political uses of the mode in the texts listed here. *One Hundred Years* is an appropriate point of departure for this comparative discussion; it is a definitive example of the mode, and several authors on the syllabus—Allende, Morrison, and Donoso—are direct beneficiaries of García Márquez's magical legacy. In this context, it is essential to link *One Hundred Years* to the historical events it encodes: critical studies by Lucila Inés Mena ("Cien años") and Stephen Minta (*García Márquez*) are useful reference works.

Interartistic analogies may be particularly interesting. The term *magical realism* was first coined in the 1920s to describe a tendency in German painting (Menton). More to the point, Latin American visual and plastic arts have traditionally proceeded as much from systems of belief (indigenous and colonial) as from empirical observation of the world. Latin American painting has often been more stylized, more visually conceptual than its European and North American counterparts. The tendency toward fantastic depiction continues today in Latin American art, as is clear in several recent exhibitions (Billeter; Day and Sturges). Thus, comparing examples of contemporary magical realism in literature and painting highlights compositional and descriptive strategies in both the visual and the verbal media. The Colombian painter Fernando Botero is a suggestive visual analogue to *One Hundred Years*, Spanish-Mexican painter Remedios Varo seems to paint the clairvoyant women in Isabel Allende's novel *The House of the Spirits*. While such interartistic analogies need not pretend to structured or systematic analysis, they do enliven and enlarge the comparative discussion of literary forms.

As I have taught comparative courses, I have recalled the late eighteenth-century debate between Joshua Reynolds and William Blake about the relative merits of the specific and the general. At the outset, one feels the strong competing claims of specificity and of generality and the urgent need to balance depth of discussion against comparative breadth, specialization against scope, exhaustive textual analysis against suggestive cultural relations. But the copious critical speculation made possible by a comparative overview highlights the specifics of texts and cultures as their contrasting features begin to emerge and take shape. Comparative literary study of *One Hundred Years* enriches the students' understanding of García Márquez's masterpiece; it also makes them more self-conscious readers and residents of the Americas.

One Hundred Years of Solitude
in History, Politics, and Civilization Courses

Chester S. Halka

One Hundred Years of Solitude offers numerous opportunities for courses on Latin American history, politics, culture, and civilization. The archetypal dimension of many of the characters provides material for discussion and study of Colombian, Latin American, and world history. Obvious parallels to events from Colombia's past are included in the novel. Moreover, history is treated thematically in the narrative. A reading of *One Hundred Years* allows for a consideration of the nature and the meaning of history and of the changes in Latin American interpretations and perceptions of its own history over time. Several critics, in fact, see Colombian and Latin American history, especially the critique of historical understanding, as the main theme of García Márquez's masterpiece. Here I consider some ways in which *One Hundred Years* includes specific events from the culture and the civilization of Latin America and from the history and the politics of Colombia. After that the question of how the novel treats history thematically is explored. Finally, the ending of the novel, as it can be related to the theme of history in the narrative, is examined. What emerges is the link between solitude and a faulty interpretation of Latin American history on the one hand and the importance of a proper historical understanding for the future of Latin America on the other hand. This essay reflects the different undergraduate contexts in which I have included the novel: courses for Spanish majors, for non-Spanish majors, and for international relations majors with a specialization in Latin America; courses in Spanish and courses in English; literature courses and courses in Hispanic culture.

Many critical studies of García Márquez and of *One Hundred Years* contain valuable material for nonliterary approaches to the novel. A good minimal preparation for approaching the work from the perspective of history, culture, civilization, and politics is to consult the studies by Raymond L. Williams, George R. McMurray, Stephen Minta, and Gerald Martin and to read García Márquez's ten-paragraph Nobel Prize acceptance speech ("Solitude of Latin America"). All are available in English. They are excellent choices for reserve readings, too, although Martin's article is less accessible than the others to undergraduates. For instructors who read Spanish, Lucila Inés Mena's study on the novel (*La función*) is also helpful for teaching it in a history, politics, or civilization course. These studies are also good sources of additional reserve readings; in them one can find such works as those by Germán Arciniegas, Charles W. Bergquist, Robert H. Dix, Vernon L. Fluharty, and Paul H. Oquist, which provide students with much pertinent information on the culture, history, and politics of Colombia. Teachers may also consider showing the film *Gabriel García Márquez: La magia de lo real*.

Some students have found it beneficial to read a short story by García

Márquez in conjunction with *One Hundred Years*. One possibility is "One of These Days" ("Un día de éstos"), a brief story that gives students an idea of how the author addresses *la violencia*, the bloody period of Colombian history from 1946 to 1966, a time of social and political upheaval that has preoccupied García Márquez, especially in his early writing. Even a three-page story like this one can give students a taste of the author's early style and can help them identify and appreciate better the historical and political concerns of García Márquez in *One Hundred Years*.

One approach to present the treatment of history, culture, and civilization in *One Hundred Years* is to have the students keep a list of who and what are introduced into Macondo in each of the first five chapters and a description of how García Márquez presents them to us. For example, discussing the acts and the significance of Melquíades in chapter 1 can provide a convenient framework for establishing Macondo as a community previously untouched by modern science, a town existing outside of Western history. The description of Macondo as "a truly happy village where no one was over thirty years of age and where no one had died" (16; 18) can get students thinking about the narrator's view of "progress" and of the desire to come into contact with the "great inventions" that transforms José Arcadio Buendía, the founder. Chapter 2 offers the exodus of José Arcadio, Ursula, and their followers "toward the land that no one had promised them," a phrase that reflects the often ironic use of biblical references in the novel (27; 31). A discussion of such references can introduce several related themes important throughout the novel, such as myth, sacred history, the relationship between history and literature, and sacred literature as a record of the history and the culture of a civilization. At a less abstract level, chapter 2 ends with the connection of Macondo to the surrounding world, which will bring commerce to Macondo. Ursula's unsuccessful search for her son José Arcadio results in her discovery of a route to neighboring settlements and in the arrival of new people.

In chapter 3 Ursula begins her own commercial enterprise in caramel animals and José Arcadio Buendía replaces the birds of Macondo with mechanical clocks. The formerly idyllic state of nature in Macondo begins to be replaced by commercialization, mechanization, and socialization. In chapter 3 politics and the first armed soldiers are also introduced to Macondo with the arrival of Apolinar Moscote and his ordinance that all houses must be painted blue, the color of the Conservative party. A more sophisticated discussion of history, culture, and civilization could compare the forgetfulness plague of chapter 3 with the treatment of pre-Columbian cultures in *One Hundred Years*. The apparent absence of indigenous cultures in the novel can be considered in the light of replacing a reality based on the immediate experience of nature with one based on the written word. The expression of indigenous experience in terms of European concepts, language, and ideas is essentially the negation of that experience. In courses where it is fitting, the opening poem from Pablo Neruda's *Canto general*, "Amor América" ("Love for America"), may be used as a basis for comparison (De Costa 108–10). Mena considers the role and the treatment of the indigenous peoples of Latin America in *One Hundred Years* in her conclusion (*La función* 199–203).

Pietro Crespi, the Italian musician and dance master, introduces European culture to Macondo in chapter 4 when he inaugurates the renovated Buendía house with a concert of waltzes on the pianola. Imported merchandise from Vienna, Holland, Bohemia, and the Indies Company also arrive with the Italian, who opens a music store. In chapter 5 the church takes hold in Macondo with the arrival of Father Nicanor Reyna, who is brought by Apolinar Moscote, the civil authority. Echoes of the installation of the government in Macondo from chapter 3 are evident in the description of the priest's response to the townspeople, who have been living "subject to natural law" and who feel no need for a spiritual intermediary, as, in their own words, "they had been many years without a priest, arranging the business of their souls directly with God" (77; 85). Students may be asked to compare how politics and the church reach Macondo and whether García Márquez's presentation of these cultural establishments colors the reader's view of them. Education, too, is brought to Macondo in this chapter; significantly, its inception is linked to politics, as it is Apolinar Moscote who succeeds in getting the government to build a school so that Arcadio Buendía can attend (81; 90). The chapter ends with the outbreak of civil war, which the heirs of the original families enter—under the leadership of Colonel Aureliano Buendía—out of personal, rather than political, considerations.

Any reading of the novel that focuses on Latin American history explores the importance of the civil war and the influence of the banana company. Both are treated at length in the narrative, and they are explicitly connected by "the solemn lawyers dressed in black":

> Also arriving on the special [train] car, fluttering around Mr. Brown, were the solemn lawyers dressed in black who in different times had followed Colonel Aureliano Buendía everywhere, and that led the people to think that the agronomists, hydrologists, topographers, and surveyors, like Mr. Herbert with his captive balloons and his colored butterflies and Mr. Brown with his mausoleum on wheels and his ferocious German shepherd dogs, had something to do with the war. (196; 213–14)

These lawyers may be compared to Pablo Neruda's *abogados del dólar* ("the dollar lawyers"), who are described in a poem by that name in *Canto general* (De Costa). With the civil war and the plaza massacre, García Márquez follows Colombian history to a degree that can surprise those students whose first impression of the novel is rooted primarily in a response to the more obvious magical realism of the work, rather than to the equally pervasive—though perhaps less obvious—social realism it contains. In view of the tone and the expression that García Márquez commonly uses to present even serious social criticism on the one hand and the initial ignorance of Colombian history that American readers routinely bring to the novel on the other, such a reaction may be understandable, but it can lead to a serious misreading of *One Hundred Years* as a delightful but ultimately fantastic set of reflections on life in Latin America. Students often need help to understand that these two realisms are entwined inextricably in the novel and that a proper understanding of the technique of magical realism, a narrative device central to *One Hundred Years*, depends on a complementary awareness and proper understanding of the social realism that informs the work. The film *La magia de lo real* is effective in conveying this idea. Within the novel a good opportunity for demonstrating the interdependence of these two realisms is provided by the episode of the massacre and its aftermath, a topic taken up below, after a brief summary of Colombian political history from 1863 to 1902 and a consideration of the striking parallels between the civil wars that racked the country and those described in *One Hundred Years*.

In spite of a narration that often laces the presentation of the war episodes in the novel with absurdity and comic overtones that seem more consonant with magical, rather than social, realism, links between Colombian history and events in the novel are strong. In 1863 in Rionegro, Colombia adopted a new constitution that embodied the ideals of the Liberal party. Rafael Núñez, a Liberal, proposed drastic changes in this constitution in 1884. As a result, the Liberal party was divided into two wings, the independents and the radicals; the independents, including Núñez, were joined by the Conservatives to provide a coalition majority. The radical Liberals, who were in the majority in their party, violently opposed the changes by going to war in 1884. They were defeated in eight months. In 1886 reforms were instituted by the ruling coalition of Conservatives and independent Liberals, and they vitiated the Liberal changes effected in 1863. Included among the reforms were a return to centralism from the federalism proclaimed in the 1863 constitution and the restitution to the Catholic church of the powers that had been taken away from it in Rionegro (Mena, *La función* 40–43). The radical Liberals, under the direction of Colonel Rafael Uribe Uribe, fought tenaciously, if sporadically and ultimately unsuccessfully, during the next seventeen years, mounting three primary uprisings in defense of the Liberal ideals that had been voted out of the constitution. The independent Liberals were the only legal representatives of liberalism in Colombia in those years. They repudiated Uribe Uribe, just as the Liberals in government positions renounce Colonel Aureliano Buendía and his wars in the novel. Students can be asked to read a biography of Uribe Uribe and to compare him with Colonel Aureliano Buendía.

Mena establishes a number of compelling parallels between the treatment of civil war in *One Hundred Years* and events during the three civil wars that occurred in Colombia between 1884 and 1902. Citing the novel, she presents the following general coincidences: in the narrative the wars last "nearly twenty years" (94, 148, 150, 172, 187; 104, 162, 164, 204); there are three clearly delimited wars (the first, 93–107; 102–116; the second, 115–30; 127–42, when the Conservative general Moncada is named magistrate of Macondo; and the third, 137–55; 149–70, with the Treaty of Neerlandia); the descriptions and actions of Colonel Aureliano Buendía parallel in many details those of Colonel Uribe Uribe; and in the novel, just as in Colombian history, the Treaty of Neerlandia ends the wars (the Treaty of Neerlandia was signed by Uribe Uribe on 24 October 1902). Other specific parallels between the Colombian civil wars and those in the novel that Mena explores include the causes, the organization, and the results of the wars; the aura of myth and legend that surrounds the real and the fictional colonels and their international reputations; and, perhaps most significant, the rejection of the two colonels and their Liberal ideals by members of their own party who compromised with the Conservatives to preserve common interests (*La función* 47–62). This point is made a number of times in the novel—for example, in the colonel's offhand remark that "the only difference today between Liberals and Conservatives is that the Liberals go to mass at five o'clock and the Conservatives at eight" (209; 228) and during a visit by a commission of the Liberal party that comes to discuss the future of the war with the colonel (147; 162). At this meeting it is clear that, in the eyes of the Liberal commission, power, not the Liberal ideals of 1863, is the motivating force behind the armed struggles, and the delegates petition the colonel to fight for the same things as his enemies, the Conservatives. Uribe Uribe, when he perceived that the armed conflict against the government was doomed to failure, fought for guarantees for the radical Liberal soldiers, just as Colonel Aureliano Buendía does, ultimately, in the novel.

Not only many similarities but also fundamental differences surface when Uribe Uribe and Colonel Aureliano Buendía are compared (Mena, *La función* 61). García Márquez's grandfather also fought in the Colombian civil wars, and he, too, served the author as a model in some particulars for Colonel Aureliano Buendía. Yet the many parallels between Uribe Uribe and Colonel Aureliano Buendía can demonstrate clearly to students an obvious desire on the part of García Márquez to include history in his novel and to do so faithfully. Aureliano Buendía represents the liberal movement in Latin America in general, not only in Colombia. The mythic and legendary proportions accorded the colonel in the litany that opens chapter 6, as well as the details of his later private life, contain elements of the ideals, attitudes, successes, and failures of populist liberalism in Latin America around the turn of the century.

In Macondo, as in Colombia, the period immediately after the Treaty of Neerlandia was marked by an economic prosperity that was largely the result of huge foreign investment, and in "the zone," as the banana-producing areas of Colombia were called, the United Fruit Company was the most powerful presence. Aracataca, García Márquez's hometown, is located in "the zone," in the Santa Marta district of the department of Magdalena. In the treatment of the Banana Company and the transformation it brings to Macondo, especially in the narration of the episode of the massacre and its aftermath, the surreal flavor given to many of the events derives directly from history. A massacre took place at the railroad station in the town of Ciénaga, which is in the same Santa Marta district as Aracataca. It occurred sometime after 1:30 a.m. on 6 December 1928, and the massacre in the novel clearly takes this event as its model (Minta 168–72; Mena, *La función* 62–85). This episode in Colombian history has received a great deal of attention and investigation, although no consensus on certain details, such as the number of dead, has ever been reached. There is agreement, however, that the government reports of the event were grossly inaccurate and purposefully misleading. Jorge Eliécer Gaitán, who became the leader of the Colombian Liberal party in the 1940s and whose assassination triggered the onset of *la violencia* in Colombia, went to Ciénaga to investigate the massacre after it occurred, and both Minta and Mena discuss his findings in relation to *One Hundred Years*. Gaitán interviewed people and in September 1929, after he had been elected to congress, he publicly denounced the government for its role in the massacre and for its attempts to cover up what had happened at the Ciénaga station. In the testimony he collected is the claim by an eyewitness that the dead and wounded were loaded into trucks and thrown into the sea or into a common grave prepared by the government troops that fired on the striking banana workers (Gaitán 56). We see, then, how one of the more fantastic details of the narration of the massacre in the novel—the two-hundred-car-long train packed with dead and wounded bodies on which José Arcadio Segundo awakes—has its precedent in the history that Gaitán presented to the Colombian congress in the aftermath of the Ciénaga tragedy. A second detail, the insistence by all the characters except José Arcadio Segundo that "nothing has happened," that "[t]here haven't been any dead" (261–62; 285), is a literary rendering of the reluctance of the people involved to discuss what had occurred out of fear for their lives.

Mena also identifies other touches of magical realism related to the banana company episodes in the novel. Among them are the supernatural powers of the engineers who move the river from one side of Macondo to the other (197; 214) and the legal decree establishing the nonexistence of the workers (256; 280). Gaitán accused United Fruit of erecting dams and dikes that altered the course of rivers in order to flood their competitors' land; the company made a successful court defense of its practice of paying less than the legal minimum wage by claiming that it had no permanent workers on its payroll, that all its laborers were hired as temporary help (Mena, *La función* 65, 69). Specific examples such as these can help students better understand how García Márquez often uses history for the germ of his magical realism, a fact he has consistently admitted (Fernández-Braso, García Márquez 65–67). Besides explicitly linking magical realism and social realism, such examples give the reader a deeper appreciation of the extent to which García Márquez includes history in *One Hundred Years* and turns insight into magical realism, one of the most characteristic devices in the novel.

The economic boom that follows the banana company to Macondo and the dramatic transformation and subsequent decay of the town when the company leaves are also accurate reflections of history. How the novel presents the magnitude and the nature of the influence of the company is a good topic for discussion, for it focuses students on what can be called true and false interpretations of history within *One Hundred Years*. This subject is treated below, when José Arcadio Segundo's understanding of the banana company and its effects on the town is contrasted with the false but universally accepted official version.

For courses dealing with history, politics, or culture, two particularly attractive characteristics of García Márquez's novel are that it gives the reader an insight into the human reality underlying historical events and that it dramatizes historical facts or concepts in character interaction. Examples abound in the book, and the three given here are representative. When Aureliano Buendía decides to oppose the Conservatives and go to war, his decision is based primarily on human, rather than political or ideological, considerations. He responds most strongly not to the imposition of martial law in Macondo but to the brutal execution of a woman who had been bitten by a rabid dog. The first act he and his men carry out after taking over the garrison in Macondo is to execute the captain and the four soldiers who had killed the woman (93; 103). In a brief passage the author communicates the presence of possible political reasons for going to war, but these are then clearly subordinated to the characterization of the rebels as persons who respond to a human outrage. This episode, in fact, accurately represents the Colombian reality; while the political lines seemed to be drawn sharply during the civil wars between 1884 and 1902, the people fighting had varying motives for their participation, and many had no clear idea of why they were fighting (Mena, *La función* 56). This last point is illustrated in the novel when a soldier responds to Aureliano José's question, "Can a person marry his own aunt?" by telling him: "He not only can do that . . . but we're fighting this war against the priests so that a person can marry his own mother" (132; 145). A second example involves a love triangle. Rebeca Buendía attracts two men: Pietro Crespi, the refined representative of European culture, whose propriety contrasts with the unbridled animal nature of the protomacho José Arcadio. This triangle can serve as a point of departure for a consideration of the famous view of Latin America popularized by Domingo F. Sarmiento, in which Latin American reality and identity are defined as the unequal struggle between civilization—that is, European culture and refinement—and a stronger impulse, barbarism. The third example deals with the responses of the townspeople to the "scientific marvels" introduced by Melquíades and to José Arcadio Buendía's "incredible" pronouncement: "The earth is round, like an orange" (12; 14). These dramatizations not only are more entertaining than a factual account of when the scientific revolution penetrated Latin America but also communicate at an emotive level, rather than a purely intellectual level, thereby leaving the reader with a better sense of the reality García Márquez successfully conveys. Moreover, each of these three examples, as is often the case with the novel, provide starting points for discussions on general themes concerned with history, culture, and civilization that extend beyond Latin America, such as national-Continental identity, societal taboos, clashing worldviews, science and nature, tradition versus spontaneity, and superego versus id.

Besides incorporating specific events from Latin American history into its pages, *One Hundred Years* also treats history thematically. The novel makes a sharp distinction between true history and false history: true history is associated with Melquíades's writings and with a nonconventional perspective; false history is linked to the official history disseminated by state propaganda and by historians approved by the government. This distinction emerges most clearly in the aftermath of the banana-company massacre. José Arcadio Segundo, locked in Melquíades's room, where he repeatedly reads the gypsy's parchment manuscripts, becomes convinced that his version of the massacre is true, even though everyone else believes the official explanation that nothing happened. Commenting on this conviction, which José Arcadio Segundo has passed on to his grandnephew Aureliano Babilonia-Buendía (who eventually deciphers the manuscripts), the narrator says:

> Actually, in spite of the fact that everyone considered him mad, José Arcadio Segundo was at that time the most lucid inhabitant of the house. He taught little Aureliano how to read and write, initiated him in the study of the parchments, and he inculcated him with such a personal interpretation of what the banana company had meant to Macondo that many years later, when Aureliano became part of the world, one would have thought that he was telling a hallucinated version, because it was radically opposed to the false one that historians had created and consecrated in the schoolbooks.   (296; 321–22)

In fact, when Aureliano finally does venture out into the world, people do argue with him, repudiating what they call "the myth of the workers hemmed in at the station" and denying that the banana company ever existed (329; 359). Significantly, the only person who shares Aureliano Babilonia-Buendía's understanding of history is a character named Gabriel, the great-great-grandson of Colonel Gerineldo Márquez—in other words, the namesake of the author of *One Hundred Years*: "Aureliano and Gabriel were linked by a kind of complicity based on real facts that no one believed in, and which had affected their lives to the point that both of them found themselves off course in the tide of a world that had ended and of which only the nostalgia remained" (329; 359).

Gerald Martin refers to the above passages to argue that *One Hundred Years* is a "demystification" of Latin America's interpretation of its own history, a "deconstructionist reading of that history" (111):

> Sarmiento's struggle between civilization and barbarism, Rodo's ex-altation of Ariel against Caliban, the sick continent diagnosed by Bunge and Arguedas, Keyserling's swamp-like dawn of creation and *tristeza criolla* (creole sadness), Martínez Estrada's view of Latin Americans as victims of a historical mirage, Mallea's incommunicability, and— above all—Mureña's original sin thesis: these and many other weird and wonderful theories of American history jostle for supremacy throughout the novel, only to find themselves circumscribed, at the last, by a conception which coincides closely with the rather more lucid kinds of perspective that emerged in Mexico after 1945, namely Paz's assertion that Latin Americans were now the contemporaries of all men and Zea's thesis that it was time, at long last, to break out of the labyrinth of solitude and assimilate the history of the continent.   (102)

Like Martin, Mena identifies history and its proper understanding as the central theme of *One Hundred Years* (*La función*; see esp. 199–218), and her entire study is devoted to validating this claim. A close reading of the final paragraphs of the novel can support the idea that an unconventional but truer understanding of history is the principal focus of García Márquez's masterpiece. The famous ending, which has received much critical comment, fascinates students, and yet they often find it bewildering. Questions that have come up time and again in classroom discussions include the following: Does Aureliano really die? What is the meaning of the identification in the closing paragraph of this character with the reader? Is the exile of the city of mirrors (or mirages) from the memory of men that is mentioned in the final sentence positive or negative? While purely literary explanations of the ending—such as the view that literature possesses a dual nature, existing simultaneously within and outside of time—are certainly germane, they ignore what the ending seems to be saying about history and historical understanding. The closing paragraphs of the novel contain at least nine events that explicitly reflect characteristics of universal initiation rituals. Such an assertion may initially seem surprising or even incongruous in a discussion of historical interpretation, but a central goal of religious rites of passage is a truer, more complete explanation of history.

The religious historian Mircea Eliade comments that tribal initiations do not describe the acts of creation by a supreme being as much as they reveal the past history of the group to the person being initiated, which is exactly what happens to Aureliano Babilonia as he deciphers Melquíades's history of the Buendía family at the end of *One Hundred Years*:

> What is communicated to the novices is, then, a quite eventful mythical history—and less and less the revelation of the creative acts of the Supreme Beings. The doctrine transmitted through initiation is increasingly confined to the history of the Ancestors' doings, that is, to a series of dramatic events that took place in the dream times. To be initiated is equivalent to learning what *happened* in the primordial Time—and not what the Gods are and how the world and man were created.   (Eliade 40; see also Halka, *Melquíades* 57–72)

As Eliade explains it, initiation is a process more closely associated with the proper understanding of group history and with individual psychology than with creation myths or with institutional religion as we know it in the West; García Márquez's use of initiatory material may be ironic, at least in part, but the parallel between Aureliano's experiences at the end of the novel and a spiritual rite of passage stresses the importance of one's understanding of history and suggests that installation in a "true" historical perspective is a process both liberating and transforming. According to Eliade, the basic theme of all forms of initiation is the ritual death and rebirth of the initiate. This fundamental motif undergoes various degrees of elaboration, he states, but is usually accompanied by at least some of the following experiences that befall the initiate: (1) a loss of consciousness; (2) tortures and suffering; (3) a ritual killing and dismemberment by a mythical agent, usually chthonic; (4) forgetting the past; (5) receiving a new name; (6) learning a new language; (7) learning the mythical history of the tribe; (8) experiencing a mystic light; and, finally, (9) the discovery that the initiate is the hero or protagonist of the ancient myths just related to him.

In the final three paragraphs of *One Hundred Years*, we can see all these elements. One of them, learning the history of his ancestors, is what Aureliano Babilonia does as he deciphers Melquíades's manuscripts. During this experience he also learns that he is the protagonist of the family history, a second element identified by Eliade, for we read, in the last paragraph of the novel, that "Francis Drake had attacked Riohacha *only so that* [Aureliano Babilonia and Amaranta Ursula] could seek each other through the most intricate labyrinths of blood until they would engender the mythological animal that was to bring the line to an end" (emphasis added). Aureliano's central role in the family saga is underscored by the fact that the history itself was to end "at the precise moment when Aureliano Babilonia would finish deciphering the parchments" (351; 383). Three more characteristics of initiatory ceremonies are depicted by other details in the final paragraph. Aureliano receives a new name, his real one, Aureliano Babilonia, as he decodes Melquíades's verses, and his act of deciphering what the gypsy has left written constitutes learning a new language, for he reads the Sanskrit in which they are written "without the slightest difficulty, as if they had been written in Spanish and were being read under the dazzling splendor of high noon" (349; 381). This last detail, that the parchments appear to be illuminated by a "dazzling splendor"—in spite of the fact, made explicit in the narrative, that Aureliano "did not have the calmness to bring them out into the light" (349; 381)—corresponds to the mystic-light experience mentioned by Eliade.

Three final elements—a loss of consciousness, suffering, and forgetting the past—are also part of Aureliano's experience in the final paragraphs of *One Hundred Years*. Aureliano apparently passes out in the town square after he has been drinking all night, for the character Nigromanta "rescue[s] him from a pool of vomit and tears" and takes him to her place, where he falls into what is described as "a dull and brief sleep" (348; 380). The cause of the suffering that leads to Aureliano's drunken stupor and subsequent loss of consciousness is Amaranta Ursula's death, and this blow is soon compounded by the horrible sight of the ants dragging the remains of his son to their burrow. Aureliano's ultimate response to all this pain is to make a conscious effort to blot out his past, an act explicitly described at the beginning of the final paragraph of the novel:

> Aureliano had never been more lucid in any act of his life as when he forgot about his dead ones and the pain of his dead ones and nailed up the doors and windows again with Fernanda's crossed boards so as not to be disturbed by any temptations of the world, for he knew then that his fate was written in Melquíades' parchments. (349; 381)

It remains to consider, in the light of the final events of the novel, what Eliade identifies as the basic motif of all initiation rites: the ritual death and rebirth of the initiate. In the penultimate paragraph of the narrative, we witness the death of a character whose parents have named him Aureliano Buendía, the infant whose remains are described as "a dry and bloated bag of skin that all the ants in the world were dragging toward their holes along the stone path in the garden" (349; 381). In the final paragraph, a character who believes he is another Aureliano Buendía discovers his true surname, and in the context of the initiatory motif of death and rebirth this is significant, for in a sense Aureliano Babilonia comes into being—or becomes aware of who he truly is—only in the final paragraph of the novel, and his only role in the novel is that of reader. What the initiatory material in the last pages of the narrative suggests is that the character who wrongly thought himself to be Aureliano Buendía dies a ritualistic death, symbolized by the death of the child with the same name; then, as in a christening ceremony, he is symbolically reborn, an act signaled by his new name, Aureliano Babilonia.

He dies as a character in the narrative to become its reader, and, as we have seen, García Márquez uses an abundance of initiatory elements to dramatize this process.

Perhaps the phrase "city of mirrors (or mirages)" in the final sentence of the novel refers to the false historical understanding that has plagued Latin America in its painful search for self-identity. The fate of "the city of mirrors (or mirages)" is to be "exiled from the memory of men at the precise moment when Aureliano Babilonia would finish deciphering the parchments" (351; 383), a fitting destiny for a false understanding, to be banished by a truer one in the same way that darkness is banished by light. Consider having your students reread García Márquez's Nobel prize acceptance speech as they finish the novel. In this terse and moving statement the author speaks of Latin America's ongoing search for its identity and defines "the nub of our solitude" as the attempt "to make our life credible" to foreigners. The next remark reinforces the idea that a radical change in the understanding of Latin America and its history is directly linked to its solitude in García Márquez's mind: "To interpret our reality through schemas which are alien to us only has the effect of making us even more unknown, even less free, even more solitary" ("Solitude of Latin America" 209). Aureliano's self-discovery in the final paragraph of the narrative—symbolized by his learning his true surname, Babilonia—is the direct result of deciphering the true history of his family. These two interrelated discoveries prepare the reader—and we should remember that Aureliano Babilonia's only role in the novel is that of reader—for a future in which solitude—the result of misunderstanding personal and family history and, by extension, regional and possibly even universal history—has been "exiled from the memory of men" (351; 383). The germ of hope that this interpretation of the ending of the novel contains is echoed in the concluding sentence of García Márquez's 1982 address in Stockholm:

> Face to face with a reality that overwhelms us, one which over man's perception of time must have seemed a utopia, tellers of tales who, like me, are capable of believing anything, feel entitled to believe that it is not yet too late to undertake the creation of a minor utopia: a new and limitless utopia for life wherein no one can decide for others how they are to die, where love really can be true and happiness possible, where the lineal generations of one hundred years of solitude will have at last and for ever a second chance on earth. ("Solitude of Latin America" 211)

One Hundred Years of Solitude in Women's Studies Courses

María Elena de Valdés

Social myths are a community's tradition of identity. They are the stories repeated by every generation until they become systems of belief or an ideology of identity. They are an essential part of history, although they are not the historical record; these beliefs are the basis for action.

The social myths of Latin America are complex hybrids of European myths and autochthonous myths of the New World, but, like all social myths, they tell the stories of beginnings and end, of chaos and order, of good and evil, in a manner that allows the community to find its distinctive sense of identity. The basic identity of not only place and language but also common past eventually becomes the most powerful determinant in the social structure of a people.

An essential aspect of the social myth is that it is a story told and retold numberless times by a multitude of storytellers. Therefore, as long as the social myth survives as a common ideology, it is a fundamental part of literary expression. Only when a social myth is dead because the community has changed its identity does literature move on to another mythological basis for the community's literature.

The central concern of this essay is to elaborate a teaching approach in women's studies that introduces the status of women in Latin America through literary texts—in particular, *One Hundred Years of Solitude*.

In women's studies I am concerned with the way Latin American women today see themselves and are seen by their community at large. The pedagogical aim is to present the ideological framework for being a woman in the world of action in the Spanish- and the Portuguese-speaking areas of Latin America. This task cannot be accomplished in one course, and literature is not the exclusive means to this end. Quite the contrary. A broadly based interdisciplinary program is the only way to meet the challenge of this topic, and literature is but one important part of the full project. The novel that concerns us here is valuable as an introduction to social myth as the basis for the ideology of identity. Consequently, my purpose here is to demonstrate how the novel's mythical structure is related to the role of women in Latin America and how this textual commentary can be used in the classroom.

I have developed this teaching approach in a seminar on women in Latin America at the Colegio de México. Literature and the Status of Women in Latin America is an interdisciplinary seminar that lends itself to team teaching by a social scientist and a literary critic. The course examines Latin American novels and theater in the sociocultural context of contemporary Latin America from a feminist perspective. The primary emphasis is placed on the portrayal of women, the use of ideology about women, and the reader response to women brought about through the reading experience.

The course brings together research on women and the status of women in Latin America and a number of significant literary texts, usually four long works. I select the literary texts for both their creative power of figuration and their reflection of reality. *One Hundred Years of Solitude* is a basic text because it offers students both an aesthetic configuration of life and an excellent presentation of social myths and female life situations, the two foundations for the course.

The three mythical elements of social identity I consider correspond to the concepts of origin and end, of order and disorder, and of common good and evil. Between them, these three social myths touch on most aspects of the community's identity.

The social myth of origin is central to the text. Macondo at the beginning of the novel draws from Genesis 2.11; things must be named because they are new, and, just as Cain and his descendants go east of Eden to dwell in the land named Wandering because Cain has killed his brother and is beset with guilt, so does José Arcadio leave after killing Prudencio and go off to start his own community. But the novel makes two notable departures from the Genesis narrative. First, while guilt has exiled Adam and Eve from Eden and has caused their son Cain to wander, in the novel José Arcadio's wandering leads to Eden-Macondo, not away from it. Second, the transgressions of Adam and Eve, disobedience, and of Cain, murder, are caused by Adam and Eve's innocence and curiosity and by Cain's envy; José Arcadio's transgression is caused by Ursula's fear of incest and, consequently, the deferment of the two cousins' sexual union. Thus, human sexuality and the woman's concern for its consequences are the central causes of the wanderings that eventually lead to the foundation of Macondo (29).

Numerous myths of beginnings are based on the wandering of the group until an appropriate place is found to begin building the community. But in the novel José Arcadio's original plan was to reach the sea across the peninsula, which he mistakenly takes to be an island, and Macondo is settled as an alternative after months of futile wandering. These mythical alterations are significant because they eliminate both divine and human plans for the community's foundation and enlarge on contingency and improvisation as basic causes and because woman's role is presented not as a secondary factor but as a first cause (31–32).

These innovations eventually lead to profound changes and to a confrontation between the patriarchal Christian view of women's bodies and of sexuality as an evil that must be rigorously suppressed in all save the reproductive function, on the one hand, and the anthropological view, on the other hand, that sexual relations between men and women represent a coming of age. This confrontation comes to the surface in the novel with the Fernanda-Petra relationship, but it is also an essential conflict in the Latin American reader. The attraction that the woman's body has for the man is presented as one of the primary forces in the development of the community. The male characters in the novel are uniformly presented as uninformed about sexual matters, and it is the women who know and take care to initiate men.

Ursula and all the other women in the novel have a sexual role to play in the development of Macondo, either to participate or to abstain from life through their sexuality. Rather than presenting a simplistic patriarchal perspective of women as revered mothers or defiled whores, the novel presents a diversity of life situations for women. How do these life situations reflect on Latin American reality? And how do they respond to the European models that have been transferred by the powerful institutions of state and church?

Latin America today and the twin institutions of power, the state and the church, must be made part of the course through parallel readings or special sessions on Latin American history (Deas, "Colombia: 1880–1930"; Bergquist), demography (Collver; *Five Studies*), economic history (D'Onofrio-Flores; McGreevey), social structures and institutions (Harkess), and family structure (Elu de Leñero). Only by re-creating what Fernand Braudel calls the history of everyday life can we appreciate and examine the novel's ideology of identity. García Márquez is not a feminist, nor is the novel a text for women about women. But it is a subversion of the patriarchal belief system that both church and state maintain in Latin America as the ideological apology for the status quo that ensures their control of political power. It is ironic that the most virulent antidemocratic actions of Latin American social institutions are committed in sacred defense of the family. This is the painful history of Latin America from Tlatelolco to the Plaza de Mayo (Kennedy).

The colonial legal structure instituted in Latin America by Spain and Portugal was a repressive code that denied basic rights to most women and continued with only superficial alteration after the Latin American republics won their independence; the legal structure was not changed significantly until the first quarter of the twentieth century. This institutional denial of civil rights to women was strongest in the urban centers and weakest in the remote areas, where legal rights of property title and land ownership were communal in nature. A review of Latin American constitutional reform during the nineteenth century reveals that the protection offered to the large landed estates is directly linked to the denial of civil rights to women; nothing would be more threatening to the control of property rights by the few than the political and legal independence of women, not only because of the laws of inheritance but also because an independent population of men and women would demand a voice in governance (Gibson). Women have been held as captives of this system because the maintenance of power required it and because the ideological system made it part of religion and nationalism (Marroquín). Thus, in Colombia, Peru, and Mexico there was no possibility of change until land ownership was altered. Macondo begins as a communal rural village of farmers—"of twenty adobe houses, built on the bank of a river of clear water" (11)—but by the end of the nineteenth century it has become part of the vast landholdings of foreign interests (214). If women had only limited traditional rights in the communal village organization at the end of the nineteenth century, they had no rights at all in the corporate enterprise of the company town.

The status of women in Latin America has been most affected by the teachings of the church about all aspects of daily life, from the injunction to obey father and husband to the view of women's bodies as the instruments of Satan for the perdition of men. These basic ideas, repeated endlessly from pulpit to confessional, are central to the widespread misanthropy of *machismo* (Gissi Bustos). The fall of Adam to feminine wiles is retold time and time again as the beginning of the soul's exile from God. *Machismo*, the belief in the natural supremacy of the man over the woman, is a cultural part of Latin America, but generation after generation of women have found the means to contain, if not defeat, this sexist bias. More victims than victors emerge in this unequal struggle, but both do emerge.

In summary, the social myth of origin in *One Hundred Years of Solitude* subverts the patriarchal myth of the community's foundation by the great man inspired by divine grace and significantly alters the myths of foundation as ordained destiny. In their place this novel establishes human fears and the response to contingency as the basis of the community. The taboo of incest in most human communities is socialized in the text; the fear of incest is both the basic dread of degeneration through the continued isolation of blood lines and the threat of social insulation. The Buendía family survives the hundred years because of the offspring of Pilar Ternera, Santa Sofía de la Piedad, and Mauricio Babilonia, who not only do not marry into the Buendía family but belong to other social classes. The Buendía women as a group represent the narrow-minded, racist, upper middle class of Latin America whose insularity from working people is the basis of the social solitude that infests the continent. The end of Macondo comes when there is no new intermixing of family lines and classes. Throughout the novel Ursula fears the birth of a child with a pig's tail; Amaranta, her daughter, is tempted by her nephew; and Amaranta's great-grandniece, Amaranta Ursula, gives birth to a deformed child fathered by her nephew, Aureliano Babilonia.

The second social myth in this novel is the establishment of order out of chaos. God the Father is portrayed as the ultimate giver of laws to Moses; thus, men have the patriarchal duty to write and enforce the laws and, in so doing, to protect their women and children. This biblical wisdom is another manifestation of the concubine status of women, and it is not related to the world of action. Men make laws that protect men's interests; only communities of both men and women can make laws that respect all its members.

In this novel the men set out to organize the community and soon tire of the effort, leaving the task to women; or they set out to change the laws and only manage to destroy each other, leaving it to women to pick up the pieces and fight the most difficult battle, that of survival in spite of men's folly. Several critics (Mena, *La función*; Minta) have demonstrated the historical accuracy of the political events in this novel, and other critics (Jesse Fernández; Eugenia Neves; Raymond L. Williams) have noted the representative depth of the day-to-day life. I would now like to outline the place of women in Macondo's civil structure and development from hamlet to company town to ghost town.

The men of Macondo search for the hidden key to the unity of all things, fight futile wars, or engage in an unabated hedonistic quest for pleasure; the women, whatever else they may do, work (14). The organization of everyday life, the organization of the community, and the sustenance of all is almost the exclusive domain of women in the Buendía household (11–12, 46, 59). The tireless efforts of Ursula are continued by a number of women who come into the family through marriage or association, but Ursula's organizational skills and stamina for work are never equaled by any of her successors. The silent Santa Sofía de la Piedad has no authority in the household. While the willful Fernanda del Carpio is able to run the household, she is dependent on the work of others. Amaranta; her adopted sister, Rebeca; and Remedios Moscote share in the work, as does Remedios the Beauty two generations later. Of the outsiders who are involved with the family, both Pilar Ternera and Petra Cotes are actively engaged in the everyday tasks of family life. The most notable decline in the family history is tied to the old age and death of Ursula, who is never fully replaced by the humble Santa Sofía de la Piedad or the haughty and often irrational Fernanda del Carpio. The women of the last generation who have the capacity for survival are never given the opportunity. Renata Remedios (Meme) and her sister, Amaranta Ursula, are strong-willed, imaginative women who are the first of the family to receive formal education and travel abroad. Meme, absent from Macondo most of her youth, is exiled to a convent in the highlands and dies there without speaking again; she was removed by Fernanda because she had sexual relations with Mauricio Babilonia, and Meme gives birth in the convent to the last reader of the manuscripts. Her sister, Amaranta Ursula, the last of the Buendía women, has inherited the love of life of her great-great-grandmother and has the will to rebuild; but after her return from Europe, Amaranta Ursula becomes her nephew's lover and dies giving birth to the last of the line. The fear of incest that had concerned Ursula and had led indirectly both to the foundation of Macondo and to her linking it to the outside world had also been evident in her daughter, Amaranta, and is finally consummated with her great-great-granddaughter, Amaranta Ursula, and her great-great-great-grandson, Aureliano Babilonia.

Only in the last quarter century has historiography proceeded beyond the reconstituted event to examine the everyday life of peoples, largely because of the work of Fernand Braudel. The historical study linking social myths to the structure of life, the social organization, and the sense of identity were not part of the historical record before Braudel's work. His last book, *L'i-dentité de la France*, finished shortly before his death in 1985, integrates social myth into the historical record. In Latin America social myth has been elaborated through literature, and historiography has not fully responded to the reality of everyday life.

The political history of Latin America is filled with reconstituted events marking the domain of power; literature has told the story again and again of the fantasy of the man-god giver of laws whom political leaders aspire to emulate as strongmen. In *One Hundred Years* the giver of laws is either a fraud or destructive of life, and the individual is unable to change the corruption of the social order. Among the few men in the Buendía family who work, José Arcadio Segundo stands out as the only one who recognizes what the women have always known, that the only way to build the community is through cooperation and the sharing of authority. The army's massacre of the banana workers brings a sudden end to the plantation workers' nascent cooperative action and demonstrates to José Arcadio Segundo that the price of failure is solitude, from which there is no reprieve save death. The relatively low profile of women in Latin American history offers clear-cut evidence of the sexist bias of a historiography that ignores the history of everyday life, in which women have been the most prominent participants.

The most repressed woman in the novel, Fernanda del Carpio, is the negative will that prevents directly or indirectly either of her daughters, Meme and Amaranta Ursula, from being able to take up the challenge of renewal. Amaranta Ursula returns when the end is almost at hand, when all but the last few inhabitants have left Macondo and the effects of neglect in the tropics are closing in on the ruins of the abandoned company town; but even the last hope of her high-spirited energy ends with death when she gives birth to the malformed child. The role of women in the social history of Latin America has yet to be explored by the historian, but the social myths of work and survival are in the novel for the student to grasp and ponder.

In *One Hundred Years* the social myth of order is not the unfolding of a divine plan; it is the complex fabric of life built up by thousands of days of work and struggle against adversity. This social order of everyday existence is carried out by the women and a handful of men who are not off fighting futile civil wars.

Much has been written about the circular structure of the novel as a history of one hundred years written before it happened by Melquíades and organized in a way that is not linear but is concentrated into one visionary instant of illumination (Eaves; Jelinski; Palencia-Roth; Segre; Siemens). Only the writing and the reading are linear. The social myth of order in this novel is, therefore, the visionary configuration of the whole history of the Buendía family into one instant of insight: life is made by men and women working together and is destroyed through isolation, solitude being the price the individual must pay for not participating (Farías). The perception of the social order as the I-other relationship and of solitude as the denial of life is attained at the end, when the thousands of days and the hundreds of pages, which have been reviewed constantly, come together as the event of understanding for Aureliano and for the reader. The reading of the novel has been our activity of hours of imaginative expansion, but the insight of understanding the unity of the whole is instantaneous.

The last of the three social myths in this novel, one of vital importance for the study of women, is the myth of good and evil. The narrative voice of *One Hundred Years of Solitude* does not overtly make value judgments, but the narration does record the creation and the destruction of life. The temporal narrative unity of the story makes this an inevitable cycle of generation, destruction, and regeneration, like the ecological cycle of a forest devastated by fire. The sense of an inevitable end is fundamental to the primordial sense of beginning with which the text opens. Characters, however, do make value judgments of what is in favor of life and what is against it, judgments that are subtly supported by the narrator's characterizations. The characters who express these values, with the exception of José Arcadio Segundo and Aureliano Segundo, are women. Female characters are also the primary sources of the expression of shame and guilt, joy and exuberance, at the spectacle of life. The most poignant contrast is between the two rivals for the attention of Aureliano Segundo—Fernanda del Carpio, his wife, who considers all traces of human sexuality as sinful, and Petra Cotes, his mistress, who revels in human sexuality as a manifest expression of life. (Dinnerstein's study of sexual arrangements is useful in the examination of human sexuality in the novel.) Petra Cotes's sexual relations with Aureliano Segundo give the novel the foremost symbol of fertility and life.

Of the five women who are encompassed within the Buendía family circle at the beginning, one stands out as the mythical birth goddess—the hedonistic Pilar Ternera, lover of the two brothers, José Arcadio and Aureliano, and mother of José Arcadio's son, Arcadio, whose offspring continue the Buendía line. Pilar Ternera embodies the mythic espousal of life. The other four women stand in marked contrast. Remedios Moscote, the child bride of Aureliano, dies in miscarriage; and Arcadio's lover, Santa Sofía de la Piedad, mother of Remedios the Beauty and the twins, becomes the silent servant of the household. The other women are Amaranta and Rebeca, her adopted sister, who become a feminine version of Cain and Abel but whose victim is the hapless Pietro Crespi. The sense of evil and the bitter legacy that the death of Pietro Crespi leaves to Amaranta are with her until the end, when she dies in a solitude of her own making.

The social myth of good and evil in this novel adheres closely to the idea of life as good and the rejection of life as evil. The sign at the entrance to Macondo during the epidemic of loss of memory declares "God exists," rather than "Jesus saves." This God does not promise a better life as a reward for suffering in this life.

The naked envy of Amaranta reaches the bitter extreme of wanting Rebeca dead and is presented as evil. Similarly, Fernanda del Carpio's willing sacrifice of another's life for the sake of appearances reaches the same magnitude of evil. On the other hand, good is presented through work, making love, and joy. In summary, the novel presents no theological foundation for good and evil, only a fundamental moral sense of the two sides of human behavior. All that favors cooperation and participation in life with another is good, and all that leads to isolation and the objectification of the other is evil.

I ask my students to prepare oral reports on two or three of the major literary texts taught in the course. *One Hundred Years of Solitude* is important because of its unique probing into the social reality of Latin America. In the oral report, the student prepares a composite portrait of one female character from *One Hundred Years* by bringing together all her traits and acts. After presenting the character in her textual configuration, the student gives a brief summary of how representative or unrepresentative the characterization is in the sociocultural reality of Latin America.

The following is a summary of the eleven principal women whose life situations have been depicted in the novel. I ask the student to link one of these life situations to the status of women in Latin America. In so doing, I suggest a case-history approach to organize the social science data. Many other facets can be profitably explored with these characters, but the focus on them as women does not detract from complementary studies of their narrative function.

Ursula, the founder of Macondo, is also the dominant character in the first half of the novel. She is the commonsense, practical, tireless woman of action who is completely devoted to the survival of her community. But she is also superstitious and has deep-seated social and racial prejudices. She succeeds in every endeavor she attempts while she has her strength. She opens up Macondo to the outside, ending its Edenlike existence, but, unlike Pandora, who unwittingly lets loose the demons, Ursula acts as the midwife to the community's regeneration as a response to her lifelong fear of incest. She is the historical memory of the family, guardian of middle-class values and conservative traditions, and provider for all throughout her life. At the outset we read: "Active, small, severe, that woman of unbreakable nerves who at no moment in her life had been heard to sing seemed to be everywhere, from dawn until quite late at night, always pursued by the soft whispering of her stiff, starched petticoats" (18).

Pilar Ternera, the love goddess who outlives all the other original inhabitants of Macondo, is always the life-force for the enjoyment of life in all its plenitude. She provides or procures sexual favors. Several Buendía generations have her support and protection; she provides a significant contrast to the Buendía women in social class, sexuality, and capacity for happiness. She has a mythical role opposed to Ursula.

Amaranta, Ursula's only daughter, lacks her mother's life-force and is consumed with envy. After Pietro Crespi chooses Rebeca, Amaranta is embittered until death and refuses marriage proposals. Her contribution to the family is to bring up a number of the Buendía children. Amaranta is the opposite in temperament of Rebeca and hates her so much that she wishes her death. This hatred, begun in adolescence, lasts until Amaranta's death. She is a typical Buendía woman, whose primary victim is herself. She represses incestuous feelings toward her nephew Aureliano José. Amaranta's life of rejection of others leads her to "weep over her solitude unto death" (158). She knows that her denial of life has resulted in evil, and, in an attempt to "make up for a life of meanness," she conceives of the idea of taking letters to the dead relatives of everyone in Macondo (261).

Rebeca, not a member of the Buendía family but adopted when she is orphaned as a child, passes through her early years as a sleepwalker under the specter of death. As a young girl, she becomes Amaranta's rival for the love of Pietro Crespi, but she marries José Arcadio, Amaranta's brother, because of his sensuality and animal strength. His mysterious death makes her a recluse; she is found dead in a fetal position.

Remedios Moscote, chosen by Aureliano as his bride before she reaches puberty, is still a child when she dies in a miscarriage. Although she dies young, in the short time she was in the Buendía house, she brought merriment to all.

Santa Sofía de la Piedad is the silent woman who works tirelessly all her life. She never asks for or receives anything; she bears Arcadio a daughter and gives birth to twins soon after Arcadio dies. This woman lives and dies unknown to others. She works for others and "dedicated a whole life of solitude and diligence to the rearing of children" (330). She lacks the ability to share with others. She is not evil and does good for others, especially for the children, but she lives in a silent solitude of nonfulfillment. She is assisted by Visitación, the silent household Indian servant.

Remedios the Beauty, daughter of Santa Sofía de la Piedad and Arcadio, goes through life without understanding her body or her sexuality. The characterization of this woman is a parody not of a person but of the religious dogma of the Virgin conceived without sin, who would be the virgin mother and whose body would never be defiled with organic decomposition. Remedios the Beauty is not a virgin mother but is assumed into the heavens in a manner reminiscent of a thousand church paintings of the assumption of the Virgin Mary. She has the body of a young woman and the mind of a child: the perfect parody.

Fernanda del Carpio, a sexually repressed woman and the descendant of impoverished colonial aristocracy, has an obsession with maintaining the appearance of what she believes to be correct comportment, which in Macondo's reality is ridiculous. A short time after her marriage to the hedonistic Aureliano Segundo, she loses him as a husband in all but name when he goes to live with Petra Cotes. Fernanda del Carpio, a prude, is the cause of constant unhappiness to members of the Buendía family. She takes her daughter off to lifelong seclusion in a convent to avoid scandal because of Meme's sexual relationship with Mauricio Babilonia; when the child of that relationship is brought to Fernanda del Carpio, she considers killing him, rather than accepting public knowledge of his parentage. She opts for the more facile route of abandonment within the household. Finally, she has such a deep-seated shame of her body that, when she is in need of medical attention, she prefers treatment by the distant telepathic doctors to physical examination by a man. She maintains order but only through the tireless efforts of Santa Sofía de la Piedad and in times of need by the generosity of Petra Cotes. Fernanda del Carpio has a son and two daughters who continue the Buendía family.

Petra Cotes is the lover of Aureliano Segundo and is devoted to him and his family. She is an enterprising, active woman who is markedly independent. She accepts Aureliano Segundo as her lover, not as her master. The most notable trait of Petra Cotes is that every time she makes love with Aureliano Segundo, the livestock they have in the barn multiply. The more she makes love, the richer he becomes. Her sexuality is transubstantiated from the ritual to nature.

Renata Remedios (Meme), a daughter of Fernanda and Aureliano Segundo, returns home from school and becomes the secret lover of the automobile mechanic Mauricio Babilonia. When Fernanda discovers the young lovers, she has Mauricio shot and takes Meme to a convent in the highlands, where she remains the rest of her life. She gives birth to a boy named Aureliano, who is brought to Fernanda by the nuns.

Amaranta Ursula, another daughter of Fernanda and Aureliano Segundo, is the last of the Buendía women. She leaves Macondo and marries Gaston in Europe. She returns to Macondo and meets Aureliano Babilonia, who she does not know is her nephew. They become lovers and have a son, the last of the line, who dies shortly after childbirth. Amaranta Ursula also dies as the novel rushes to its conclusion. She has traits of her great-great-grandmother Ursula in her enthusiasm and sense of adventure, but she has also inherited the danger of incest from her great-grandaunt Amaranta. She finally gives birth to the deformed child Ursula had feared. The last of the line is born with a pig's tail. Amaranta Ursula was the last hope for the renewal of the family line, but the prudery of Fernanda takes its final victim when Amaranta Ursula takes her nephew as her lover and the father of her child.

Prostitutes are a part of Macondo. For example, the nameless mulatto girl, the model for Eréndira, is a traveling prostitute who receives sixty men a day to repay her grandmother for the loss of her house. These prostitutes are one facet of Macondo's life and, with few exceptions, are not characterized, for the boisterous Pilar Ternera fills this life situation.

This brief review of the women of *One Hundred Years of Solitude* brings out a number of important features of the novel. First, keeping a home, making a place to live, getting food, preparing meals, having children, taking care of children, and being companions and sexual partners to their mates are the sole domain of women. Men do not concern themselves with the requisites of everyday life. In this novel the women and the children even work the fields because the men are preoccupied with war or alchemy. Second, the real leadership of the community is provided by its women, from Ursula to Amaranta Ursula.

Vast areas of social interaction are involved in the life situations of the female characters of *One Hundred Years*. Sociological studies (Aguiar; Elu de Leñero; Harkess) are essential. Historical research on the laws of Colombia sheds much light on the sociocultural reality of women in Latin America. Gibson's study of the constitutions of Colombia is a valuable source. The relations of church and state must be examined because of the importance of the church in the status of women in Latin America. Studies by Guerra and Marroquín are useful. The economic history and analysis of Latin America can be studied in works by D'Onofrio-Flores and McGreevey and in *Five Studies on the Situation of Women in Latin America*. Dinnerstein's feminist study of female sexuality is a fundamental source of commentary and is supported by vital statistics on birth rates prepared by Collver, Chaney, and the Commission on the Status of Women report of 1975. Some insight into the belief systems of the nineteenth century helps outline the patriarchal ideology (Jaramillo Uribe). A journal on developments in the status of women—*fem.*—and an annotated bibliography on women in Latin America (Knaster) are helpful research tools.

A number of questions about the social myths of the novel and their reflection of the status of women in Latin America can help develop the student's research. The main topics developed in my course are women and the law, women in the work force, literacy and the education of women, social ideology, and sexism in Latin America. The questionnaire that follows facilitates student research into the social reality of women through the figurative creations of literature. Each student's paper is an individual research project on an approved topic from one or more of the literary texts, but the questionnaire helps get students immediately involved in the research.

1. What is the distribution of labor between men and women?
   What is the distribution according to the data on human geography?
   How has this distribution changed in the last century in urban and rural
      areas?

What is the distribution of labor in the novel?

What are the reasons for the distribution of labor in the novel and in Latin America?

2. What changes in the social structure have been brought about because of armed conflict?

What is the historical record of armed conflict in Latin America in the past century?

How is the historical record reflected in the novel?

What was the social structure before and after armed conflict in Latin America and specifically in Colombia and in the novel?

What are the causes of armed conflict in the history of Colombia and in the novel?

What has been the role of women in armed conflict and its aftermath in Colombia and in the novel?

3. What authority do women have in the local community?

Under what conditions and where in Latin America have men and women shared political authority?

What kinds of social but noninstitutional forms of authority exist in local communities in Latin America?

What kinds of authority do women have in Macondo?

How have the traditional roles of women as wives, mothers, mistresses, and prostitutes affected their gaining of authority in Macondo and in Latin America?

4. What authority do women have in the macrosocial institutions of national government and church? Why are women excluded from all authority in these institutions?

5. What effect has foreign involvement in Latin America had on the status of women?

How have foreign companies changed the standards of living of the local populations in their Latin American holdings?

What social changes accrue to Macondo because of the banana plantation?

After the involvement of the banana company, do Macondo women's health, education, and welfare reflect the historical record?

The primary function of literature is to help readers look at their own world again, describe it to themselves again, and evaluate it once again. This reconsideration of the social, historical, and economic reality of women is before us because we have read the novel from a feminist perspective, which should never be incompatible with the study of the novel as a work of art. My aim is not merely to understand the novel as part of the mythic social configuration of communal identity in Latin America but also to redescribe our views about the world of these women, which is our world.

One Hundred Years of Solitude
in Interdisciplinary Courses
Sandra M. Boschetto

In the spring of 1987, Michigan Technological University's Department of Humanities was awarded a three-year curriculum development grant from the National Endowment for the Humanities to strengthen its advanced foreign language and intercultural studies program.[1] The primary focus of the grant project was the design, development, and implementation of three interdisciplinary team-taught seminars beyond the third year of language and literature study. These seminars were designed primarily to increase the students' exposure to literature, the arts, and world cultures and problems with a historical perspective and to include both distributive and integrative work. The first of the advanced foreign language seminars, Technology in Literature, was initiated in the spring of 1988.

The objective of the Technology in Literature seminar is to help students understand the relation between modern technological systems and the arts as they reflect and influence culture. Through an examination of modern and contemporary literary masterpieces across languages and cultures, students study the role that technology and technological ideologies play in literary works. Technology in Literature focuses specifically on literature, film, and other selected arts from French, German, and Hispanic language communities. Its integrative theme is an investigation of how literature reflects, depicts, and often provides a critique of industrialization, mechanization, and other aspects of technology in modern society. Within the integrative theme, students also study such subthemes as machine as metaphor, utopia-dystopia, and time and space.

Courses at Michigan Technological University are taught on the ten-week quarter system. Technology in Literature is divided into three units of three weeks each, one subtheme to a unit, with the final week devoted to general conclusions and consolidations of subthemes. During each three-week sequence, incorporating six 1½-hour class sessions, three days were in the target language—with French, German, and Hispanic language groups meeting individually to discuss and analyze themes, texts, and films in the original languages—and three days in English, when all groups reported. While all students were required to read the texts outside their languages in English translation, the small groups read the texts in the original language and also discussed the texts in this language. This structure served as our model for the intercultural approach to the study of language and literature, but the semester system would provide an even better avenue for in-depth integration of both theme and subthemes.

Since the concept of world construction is operational at various levels of language, film and other visual media are used to help students gain a better understanding of the interrelation between print and visual language. Through the study of film and other visual texts, students acquire additional perspectives and interpretations of a printed text. They also study and learn how various conventions, cultural and structural—that is, time and space —operate in film and the other visual arts.

One of the aims of the seminar is to encourage students to reflect on the interrelation between translation and interpretation. Indeed, one of the problems of intercultural communication is translation. By considering translation, students learn that translators must not only translate the work but also translate the audience, restructuring interpretation in another language while trying to approximate the original structure. As readers go about the business of translating the texts they read, mingling the original with their personal expressions and social context, they create new expressions, new texts, and new translations. The instructor is encouraged to assign in each language-specific section one work that is read in English translation by all students. This sort of interlanguage comparison is particularly useful for illustrating the methods and the failures of translators. In Gabriel García Márquez's *One Hundred Years of Solitude*, as Anibal González has shown, translation is itself an intertextual concern in the novel.

As students interact with one another, confronting new value systems, challenging their assumptions, and revising their judgments, they do so as members of a community of peers and scholars committed equally to the stuggle of communicating a text and challenging individual assumptions in that struggle. In this interactive community students learn that reality is a cultural and social as well as a linguistic construction.

Technology in Literature engages students with primary texts that nurture and sustain lifelong engagement with the humanities. We select texts and films that play a clear role in the development of problem-solving skills and values formation.

Gabriel García Márquez's *One Hundred Years of Solitude* offers its readers the opportunity to explore problems pertaining to Third World development, history, political ideology, and ethics, as well as issues relating to industrialization in low-technology cultures. As some critics have already noted, the novel also serves as a metaphor for the history of humankind and of Latin America specifically. García Márquez's novel develops and expands on the three subthemes of the integrative umbrella—machine as metaphor, utopia-dystopia, and time and space—in a holistic fashion.

For the target-language group, we use the Editorial Sudamericana edition. The Harper and Row edition and the paperback Avon edition translated by Gregory Rabassa were read by all students, including those in the French and German sections.

In some ways *One Hundred Years* can be seen as a parody of the bildungsroman or, more precisely, as a parody of any number of Romantic and post-Romantic works of literature and philosophy, from Georg Wilhelm Friedrich Hegel's *Phenomenology of the Spirit* to José Vasconcelos's *La raza cósmica,* in which the learning process is seen not only in individual terms but as a collective, racial enterprise. The strong biblical metaphors and references in the novel are a reflection of the author's cultural framework and of a prehistorical or preindustrial innocence. Before the modern period the Judeo-Christian culture presumed that God had written the book of nature and that verbal symbols and metaphors incarnated the things they named. The poet was instrumental in setting forth divine analogies of God's world. This view is prefigured in the arcadian epoch of Macondo: "The world was so recent that many things lacked names, and in order to indicate them it was necessary to point" (11). Modern literature, however—and *One Hundred Years* is no exception—records the history of the breakup of this union of man, God, nature, and language. Industrialization, the rise of science and technology, urbanization, and the rise of the middle class all led to the sense of isolation and destitution experienced by the Victorian writers and those who followed them.

García Márquez portrays two worlds in the novel, one romantic and mystical and the other reflective of brutal sociocultural economic realities. Here I approach the novel as a study in the history of technology. *One Hundred Years* sharpens the contrast between classical Western models of industrialization as described by the developed countries' historians and the process characteristic of Latin America. García Márquez's novel also shows how the writer of romantic allegiances represents a constructed world of component machines and structures.

Within the target-language group, I begin by asking students to explore a series of minithemes or questions appropriate to our mutual undertaking: (1) a definition of technology, (2) technology as historical destiny (Does history shape technology, or does technology shape history?), (3) the compatibility of technology with democratic politics and economics (Are science and technology democratizing? What role does the introduction of technology and industrialization play in a low-technology culture?).

As the students explore these questions, they experience considerable confusion over what technology means. This same confusion existed in previous eras. The term *technology* had been in use since the seventeenth century to describe the practical arts. Scholars commonly infer it from such nineteenth-century American expressions as *inventions, devices, engines,* and *machines* and in Amos Eaton's "application of science to the common purpose of life" (qtd. in Iannone 27, 35; see also Meier).

The gypsies who invade Macondo with their gadgetry may parody the period of exploration, discovery, and conquest of the New World, but the inventions they introduce have no practical purpose. Catapulted from the sixteenth century into the late eighteenth century (the magnet and the telescope are symbols of the two pillars of Newtonian physics) and the nineteenth century (the train and the telegraph), the characters of the novel are unable to bring themselves into focus in a world they have not made. José Arcadio and the townspeople of Macondo are viewed as marginalized from this technological and scientific community. José Arcadio laments to Ursula: "We'll never get anywhere. . . . We're going to rot our lives away here without receiving the benefits of science" (21). Students cannot but admire the indefatigable determination with which José Arcadio proceeds to invent his world, even though every effort ends in failure or a mere copy of previous inventions. When with the help of Melquíades's instruments José Arcadio discovers that the "earth is round, like an orange," Melquíades "gave public praise to the intelligence of a man who from pure astronomical speculation had evolved a theory that had already been proved in practice, although unknown in Macondo until then" (14). José Arcadio even dreams of a flying machine that will outdo the gypsies' "miserable bedspread" (38).

It becomes apparent to the students that Macondo's underdevelopment is a consequence of development elsewhere. In Eduardo Galeano's phrase, the reason the "Goddess Technology does not speak Spanish" is that Latin America is condemned to suffer the technology of the powerful, which attacks and removes natural raw materials, and is incapable of creating its own technology to sustain and defend its own development. Macondo is merely a reflection of Latin America's predicament. Macondo's underdevelopment is not a stage on the road to development but the counterpart of development elsewhere; the region "progresses" without freeing itself from the structure of its backwardness. This may explain the numerous anachronisms in the novel—technological and scientific artifacts that make their appearance alongside more primitive ones (flying carpets, an alchemist's laboratory)— and the responses of the Macondians to the technological and scientific curiosities introduced by the gypsy tribes, responses that vary from bemused contemplation to suspicion, ambivalent acceptance, and rejection.

Symbols of prosperity are no more than symbols of dependence. García Márquez's narrator humorously deflates the prosperity achieved by the Macondians when Ursula decides to import artifacts from abroad to decorate the house for the reception she has planned to honor the founders and their families (64). Technology becomes a visible symbol of both economic and psychological colonialism. Artifacts and inventions are received as the railroads will be later—at the service of foreign interests that model and remodel the colonial status of Macondo and Latin America.

Machine images in *One Hundred Years* serve the fictional techniques of characterization, description, and evocation of mood. What the student perceives on the surface, however, is a fundamental bias against technology. José Arcadio's experiments are termed "harebrained undertakings" (80). The electric bulb, the cinema, and the telephone are all described as "mechanical trick[s]" (212). Fernanda del Carpio and her daughter Meme board a riverboat, "the wooden wheel of which had a sound of conflagration and whose rusted metal plates reverberated like the mouth of an oven" (274). This infernal image of disintegration and decay parallels the sense of foreboding inherent in the image of the "innocent yellow train" that, first heralded as "[s]omething frightful, like a kitchen dragging a village behind it," brings to Macondo "so many ambiguities and certainties, so many pleasant and unpleasant moments, so many changes, calamities, and feelings of nostalgia" (210). This is the same yellow train that arrives with an extra coach, the "mausoleum on wheels" for Mr. Jack Brown, and "with a nocturnal and stealthy velocity" finally delivers the massacred peasants for dumping into the ocean (285).

Science and technology cannot be understood outside their connection with the cultural and historical universe in which they function. This is particularly true of the Latin American model, in which technology is fundamentally biased toward domination. The railroads formed what Galeano calls a "cage of dependency" linking the control of dominated areas. "The tracks," he writes, "were laid not to connect internal areas with one another, but to connect production centers with ports. The design still resembles the fingers of an open hand: thus railroads, so often hailed as forerunners of progress, were an impediment to the formation and development of an internal market" (218). Frank Safford's *Ideal of the Practical: Colombia's Struggle to Form a Technical Elite* is another investigation into the dominant social values in Latin America, which continue to obstruct economic development there. He cites three problems, which are also echoed in the literary text: a difficult geography, a rigid social structure, and the outdated stock of scientific and technical knowledge.

The machines in *One Hundred Years*, like the "innocent yellow train," are themselves ambivalent images. The target of the criticism is, in reality, technical reason. Technology may still represent for García Márquez the hypothetical possibility of overcoming scarcity and the conflict to which it gives rise, but capitalism, as Herbert Marcuse has described, represses the technical potential for emancipation by casting society in an ever-renewed struggle for existence. The Latin American author could argue that, in a liberated society, technology as a whole contributes to freedom by serving basic needs in a new way. But this is precisely what is not present in Macondo. The critique of merchants and their commerce is apparent in the mercantilistic circus atmosphere that progresses with the arrival of the magical ice, when the use value of objects is replaced by the exchange value of trinkets. The ice factory that Aureliano Triste creates as if out of a dream—"that José Arcadio Buendía had dreamed of in his inventive delirium" (206)—is exchanged by his brother Centeno for a sherbet warehouse: "Aureliano Centeno, overwhelmed by the abundance of the factory, had already begun to experiment with the production of ice with a base of fruit juices instead of water, and without knowing it or thinking about it, he conceived the essential fundamentals for the invention of sherbet" (209–10). The town is soon overtaken by the "tricks" of other "ambulatory acrobats of commerce" (212) including the "gringos," who bring with them "a colossal disturbance, much more than that of the old gypsies, but less transitory and understand-able" (214). The "intricate stew of truths and mirages" (212) that convulses Macondo with the arrival of the merchants is echoed in Eduardo Galeano's *Open Veins*: "But hallucinations do not fill stomachs. The city makes the poor even poorer, cruelly confronting them with mirages of wealth to which they will never have access—cars, mansions, machines as powerful as God or the Devil—while denying them secure jobs, decent roofs over their heads, full plates on the midday dinner table" (270). Through ingenious irony, García Márquez points up the dualistic contradictions of a reason that prom-ised liberation and delivered a new form of domination.

In *One Hundred Years* the assumptions of the industrial revolution emerge as just that—a set of assumptions. García Márquez's readers learn to see them as formulations of reality and not as reality itself. In studying these assumptions, we investigate an era's perception. The readers of *One Hundred Years* can study an outlook on the world and recognize that certain imagi-native forms are cognate with it. Magical realism, for example, can be un-derstood as a challenge not so much to conventions of literary realism as to basic assumptions of modern positivistic thought: a critique of the vanity of Western civilization and an understanding of cultural relativity.

The political turmoil that continues to cloud Latin America has helped nourish a skepticism about the values of the industrial revolution. As students are confronted with this skepticism in *One Hundred Years*, they may confront other questions. Does history shape technology, or, as appears evident from the Latin American model, does technology shape history? This question is important for developing an overview of the significance of technology in Latin America and for understanding nineteenth- and twentieth-century Western ideology, with its conscious effort to invest technological progress with democratic legitimacy. The historical inevitability accorded technolog-ical "progress," particularly by the nineteenth-century positivists, is prob-lematic in a society such as Macondo (Latin America), which perceives divine purpose as the prime mover in the unfolding of national history. The ability to predict the future presupposes some conception of rational historical causation. But with the progressive waves of gypsies—who are viewed as symbols of advancing technology and its parent, scientific progress—this conception is lost in Macondo. Events are inexplicable, and people are the playthings of fortune. "It was as if God had decided to put to the test every capacity for surprise and was keeping the inhabitants of Macondo in a per-manent alternation between excitement and disappointment, doubt and rev-elation, to such an extreme that no one knew for certain where the limits of reality lay" (212).

Technology is presented as an irrational force that appears to have been substituted for an otherwise failed sense of history—that is, of logic and purpose in the unfolding of events. The environmental degradations per-petrated by the gringos are consistent with this view: "Endowed with means that had been reserved for Divine Providence in former times, they changed the pattern of the rains, accelerated the cycle of harvest, and moved the river from where it had always been and put it with its white stones and icy currents on the other side of the town, behind the cemetery" (214). If technology or technical reason shapes history, the logic of history is inherently technological or comprehensible through quantification and mechanical principles or analogies. Its ontology in *One Hundred Years* is likened to an intricate mechanical contrivance, devoid of spirit, taking its energy not from immaterial life forces, whether animal or divine, but from synergism, a principle derived from metallurgy. The tendency to see all things as system, a technologically related concept itself, is echoed in José Arcadio's discovery that the "time machine has broken" (81), in Ursula's sensation of the "progressive breakdown of time" (230), and in Pilar Ternera's realization that "the history of the family was a machine with unavoidable repetitions, a turning wheel that would have gone on spilling into eternity were it not for the progressive and irremediable wearing of the axle" (364). It is almost as though the marvelous inventions of the gypsies had acquired an aggregate identity and intelligence of their own, transforming technology into an uncertain and sinister master of human destinies.

Science and technology, as viewed from the perspective of the Third World, have not been democratizing. Instead, science and technology are linked to political rhetoric and oppression. This impression is conveyed early on in the novel when José Arcadio conceives the timely idea of using the magnifying glasses as weapons of solar war: "José Arcadio Buendía promised to undertake it as soon as the government ordered him to so that he could put on some practical demonstrations of his invention for the military authorities and could train them himself in the complicated art of solar war" (13). With the appearance of advanced science, the spirit of social initiative in Macondo disappears. Faith in progress is betrayed. Scientific discoveries mystify the citizens of Macondo, then lead to their exploitation. (A film that echoes the relations of technology, imperialism, and military dicatorship is Gregory Nava's *El norte*. The film also raises political questions about democracy and national destiny in a technological society, particularly within the framework of Third World conceptions of reality. The film helps the student visualize the conflicts present in *One Hundred Years*.)

A close reading of the novel allows both students and the instructor the opportunity to explore broader definitions of technology, which include tools and "the application and organization of knowledge" (Iannone 29). This definition incorporates language and the applications of language to the attainment of power. Technology as energy and devices, represented in the nineteenth-century images of the dynamo and the locomotive, gives way in *One Hundred Years* to the twentieth-century notion of technology as effective intelligence. In this world both the universe and the human beings who populate it are viewed in mechanistic terms. This is particularly evident in the depiction of various characters in the novel. The indecipherable Amaranta, who weaves then unweaves her shroud, afraid of love, beguiled by death; Colonel Aureliano Buendía and his endless circle of goldfish; and Fernanda del Carpio, whose circle of rigidity and unimaginative mind catapults Macondo toward its inevitable demise, are just a few of the characters who are perceived in mechanistic terms. Whatever their category, they are presumed to be mechanical—if not in form, at least in operation.

Technology as effective intelligence is also undermined in José Arcadio's attempt to construct the memory machine during the insomnia plague. This invention appears during Macondo's greatest crisis of knowledge. Language is also a technique, a tool of knowledge. The machine that the patriarch invents is designed to capture a "reality that was slipping away, momentarily captured by words, but which would escape irremediably when they forgot the values of the written letters" (53). The passage goes on to say that "keys to memorizing objects and feelings" were created. In the case of Macondo these keys are meant to facilitate, in a fixed and mechanical way, the passage between language and reality. José Arcadio's task is none other than to save reality. The immensity of the effort is further underscored by the fact that it is the same memory machine that he "had desired once in order to remember the marvelous inventions of the gypsies" (54). The machine is a kind of invention of inventions, reminiscent of the catalog of catalogs sought by the librarians in Jorge Luis Borges's "Library of Babel." The memory machine is a way to save all reality and a way to control it. Indeed, the machine was conceived during the plague to put at one's disposal nothing other than "the totality of knowledge acquired during one's life" (54).

José Arcadio "knew" what he divined, intuited, and perceived through the primitive awe of magic and superstition; at the conclusion of the novel, Aureliano Babilonia is master of all that has ever been known. He is the cumulative totality of humanity's conscience and science. He knows because, as he explains his all-embracing precognition, "Everything is known" (352). This irrefutable, absolute knowledge has led to the technicalization of life in Macondo.

The repeated arrivals of the gypsies and their heirs, the gringos, bring chaos into Macondo: instability, disintegration, dissolution. Borrowing language from technology and science, these chaotic energies exceed all human efforts at order and discipline. Instability, shown in the endless cycle of wars fought by Colonel Aureliano Buendía, corrupts and dissolves the family. The characters themselves are not immune from these negative aspects of technicalization. Instability also takes hold of the characters and is manifested in personality flaws. The most oppressive characters in the novel, in fact, appear armed with the utilitarian, industrial-age qualities of efficiency and energy. Yet, as with Fernanda del Carpio, García Márquez and his narrator are able to uncover the brutal human energies masked by this rational technological efficiency and to reveal the raging, destructive force behind the mask and the inordinate passions it conceals.

García Márquez also criticizes waste, another utilitarian, industrial-age term. *Waste* is often defined as the failure to meet functional criteria. As the contrary of efficiency, *waste* means dysfunction and danger. In technological terms, waste also presupposes intellectual analysis of a condition or situation. The analysis must include a breaking-down, a disassembly of the way something works. One of the most humorous episodes in *One Hundred Years*, an episode that demythologizes this type of analysis, is Mr. Herbert's experiment on the banana:

> Then he took a small case with optical instruments out of the toolbox that he always carried with him. With the suspicious attention of a diamond merchant he examined the banana meticulously, dissecting it with a special scalpel, weighing the pieces on a pharmacist's scale, and calculating its breadth with a gunsmith's calipers. Then he took a series of instruments out of the chest with which he measured the temperature, the level of humidity in the atmosphere, and the intensity of the light. It was such an intriguing ceremony that no one could eat in peace as everybody waited for Mr. Herbert to pass a final and revealing judgment, but he did not say anything that allowed anyone to guess his intentions.   (213)

The critical mind of Mr. Herbert has thus worked according to the defining technology of what Cecilia Tichi calls the "gear-and-girder world." The banana has been judged wasteful because, in dismantling it into its parts, the critic has recognized a more effective or efficient means by which it can operate. The eating of the banana may in this sense be viewed as wasteful. To call it wasteful is to say that it needs to be redesigned, and the critic who thinks and judges in this way is working as an engineer. Mr. Herbert perceives a world in which things and social organizations are complex assemblies subject to dismantling into components. Improvement of that world necessitates redesign part by part, eliminating the unnecessary or wasteful parts and recombining the others. To recognize the broad-based cultural response to waste is to gain an understanding of the foundation of that functional aesthetic, one based on the values of engineering and machine technology.

Among more than a dozen definitions of *waste* listed in the *Oxford English Dictionary*, one that takes a prominent place in the lexicon of *One Hundred Years* is "[t]o fail to take advantage of." In this meaning *waste* becomes the unrecognized opportunity, the missed chance for some order or gain. This summons, however, leads to threat. Disinheritance, deceit, truncated pleasures, estrangement—these terms characterize familial waste in the novel.

People of integrity and sensitivity are crushed like rotten fruit, wasted by parasites and opportunities before reaching their full powers. The protagonists of the novel are victimized by the waste of time and the waste of spirit in family relationships, business dealings, sex, politics, and war.

As another value embodied in machine technology, efficiency, the axial contrary of waste, is also parodied in *One Hundred Years*. The moral terms that cluster around *efficiency*—such as character, competence, energy, hard work, and success—are diluted as the Buendía household comes under the control of Fernanda del Carpio, who incorporates efficiency into the concepts of mastery and tyranny and who suggests that efficiency is as much the enemy of spontaneity and romance as it is the substitute for introspection and intellect. "Efficiency" becomes an ideological armament by which the vested interest victimizes and seeks control over the disenfranchised.

García Márquez's writing also depicts the influence of technology and science on the artistic medium itself. A fascinating issue raised by the novel is the veritable bridging of art and technology. The novel could, in fact, become required reading in a course dealing with literature in technological and scientific society.

The laws pertaining to theories of thermodynamics, space-time fields, bifurcation, and entropy are readily ascertainable in the novel when exploring the metaphors of time and space and their functions within the text. Einstein's notion that the shortest distance between two points is a curve is demonstrated in García Márquez's curved time model created by the mixture of primitive (circular) and biblical (linear) time.

The science of chaos—which, according to N. Katherine Hayles, includes work on nonlinear dynamics and focuses on systems whose behaviors are deterministic yet unpredictable—is also represented in *One Hundred Years*. The concern with chaos in the novel is at once thematic, social, psychological, and literary. The text may be perfectly coherent on one level and on another level, chaotic. The novel may afford the reader a new understanding of chaos, which is not always the opposite of order. Rather, as Hayles notes: "it is a repository of infinitely rich information, a precursor from whose surplus information order derives. It is *because* the system is initially perceived as disordered that a more complex kind of order can emerge. Thus chaos is not order's enemy but its partner" (12).

We are reminded here of Roland Barthes's comment on the Eiffel Tower. On approach, he says, pure line gives way to the perception of "countless segments, interlinked, crossed, divergent." The appearance of "the straight line [or, in the case of the wheel, of the circle or ellipse] becomes its contrary reality, a lace-work of broken substances" (qtd. in Tichi 143). Barthes understands this close-up perceptual change to be a demystification. The reader of *One Hundred Years* is challenged to arrive at a similar change in perception through close reading of the mechanisms underlying García Márquez's novel.

Finally, the machine itself appears to give García Márquez the example of simultaneous, continuous motion within a comprehensive, ordered, and disordered system. His method is like the photographic and cinematic montage that enabled him to achieve simultaneity in the predominantly linear form of the novel. Ambiguities are everpresent in this novel. While severely criticizing a world in which people are so vulnerable to sociocultural forces that they function virtually as interchangeable parts, García Márquez's novel is a marvel of integrated structure. The Colombian author mirrors a conception of art as structure with a framework and various fixed and moving parts intended to transmit energy. Even though he disliked its political implications, this model for fictional structure is irresistible to him.

The exemplary figure of centralized control of a complex mechanism is Melquíades, whom students may view as the inscrutable technocrat. Corporate capitalism, with its centralized control and its ethos of mass production, repelled García Márquez. However, to achieve the omniscience required for the novel, he found it necessary to participate in the power center of that structure.

While attempting to preach a romantic worldview and an organic construction, the text is a constructed world, not one of divine immanence. García Márquez encompasses personal history and the history of his time in fiction, all the while remaining true to the conviction of a disjunctive, impersonal world. As a writer with a romantic worldview, García Márquez represents his discourse in the forms of the circle and the spiral, which, in the romantic conception of history, described the steady enlargement and progression of human society through time. In an age of machine production and speed, however, these forms are rejected in favor of the straight line. But in García Márquez's novel, order and disorder function as partners. Curved talk or discourse repetition, with its minimum efficiency of expression, is counterbalanced by the syntax of the straight line, which compresses space and collapses time, thereby enacting industrial-age speed. García Márquez is full of nostalgia for a preindustrial natural environment, but his sentences are irrevocably of the gear-and-girder world. The effect of speed, developed by the text and sensed by the reader, is represented in the immediacy of the constructed reality of Macondo, a textual reality that jams words together and deluges the reader with simultaneous stimuli. This speed accelerates to such a degree in the final pages of the novel that the reality of the text and that of the reader are shattered to produce a new construction, the novel we hold in our hands. García Márquez's novel *One Hundred Years of Solitude* thus shows how it is that literature can ultimately embody the values of machine technology and exhibit a machine aesthetic, even when machines or structures play no part in the fiction or contradict the political ideologies of the author.

At the conclusion of the course, the students' definition of culture has been broadened to include both the technological-scientific and the literary-humanistic. While García Márquez's novel does not resolve the conflict between these two cultures, it mediates the ongoing debate through literary representation and a sociological-historical point of view. With the help of culturally guiding motives and an interdisciplinary perspective, *One Hundred Years* may succeed in raising students' collective consciousness to the everclosing gaps between art and technology.

NOTE

[1]The three-year grant award was issued under the project title "Strengthening Foreign Language and Intercultural Study at Michigan Technological University (1987–90)," written and directed by Sandra M. Boschetto. I thank the National Endowment for the Humanities and my colleagues Diane Shoos and Dieter Adolphs, without whose assistance the project development at Michigan Technological University and this research would not have been possible. I also extend my appreciation to John Flynn, whose Ethics in Technology course provided much of the initial stimulus and inspiration for this essay.

One Hundred Years of Solitude
in Latin American Literature Courses

Walter D. Mignolo

Because teaching literature in foreign language and literature departments is usually ancillary to teaching the language, undergraduate foreign language majors rarely have the opportunity to study literature as an academic discipline, rather than as a language-learning medium. I teach Latin American literature at the undergraduate level with two major and interrelated goals for the foreign literature curriculum: first, to affirm the principle of teaching literary studies as a discipline, instead of using literature to improve the students' linguistic skills or to acquaint them with a foreign culture, and, second, to engage students in a critical examination of cultural structures and the social, ideological, and intellectual barriers in communication across cultural boundaries. These two goals can be achieved if we train students to think critically about the function of literature in human societies and to realize that we are living in a world that is becoming a multilingual and pluricultural global village. In the analysis of discourses, we demonstrate linguistic and semiotic interactions and conflicts between race, community, class, and gender, as well as cultural traditions.

I have these basic goals in mind when planning courses on Latin American literature in translation for third-year students and courses on the contemporary Latin American novel for fourth-year and graduate students. Eliminating anthologies from the outset, I stress the direct reading experience of complex texts. I often include Rigoberta Menchú's *Me llamo Rigoberta Menchú y asi nació mi concienca* (*I . . . Rigoberta Menchú: An Indian Woman in Guatemala*) and Rudolfo Anaya's *Bless Me, Ultima* with *One Hundred Years of Solitude*. Menchú, who learned Spanish when she was twenty-one, narrates the experiences of a Quiché community; Anaya writes in English about people of Mexican origin. By contrasting *One Hundred Years of Solitude* with such novels and narratives, we open the doors to a critical examination concerning the aesthetic, national, linguistic, and ideological aspects of our commonsense idea of literature and its hierarchical organization.

To elaborate on the notion of cultural differences and to encourage students to begin thinking critically about them, I provide examples from Miguel Fernández-Braso's 1972 interview with García Márquez and from the novel. In the interview García Márquez said that, although he conceived of the idea of the novel at an early age, he did not know how to solve the problem of erasing the lines that divided the real from the fantastic. He found the solution when he realized that events had to be told in the same tone that his grandfather used when he told stories: to narrate incredible events in a natural tone. These remarks by García Márquez can be examined when reading the balanced chroniclelike mode of narration from the first page. I also point out to the students that the literary convention of Melquíades's manuscripts has important implications about writing and reading. We then discuss the characters' writing and reading the parchments as an analogue of García Márquez's writing and our reading the novel.

Let me expand on each of these examples. The first describes different kinds of communicative situations. Often the first definition of communication that comes to mind is the transmission of meaning and messages. I present the students the alternative conception of communication as a domain of social interactions in which signs are exchanged (which we agree to call the "domain of semiotic interactions") to coordinate and regulate social life. Communication means, primarily, common-union. At this point the students are invited to reflect on their own activities when they communicate. They are asked whether they think they are passing or transmitting something to each other when they engage in a dialogue or whether they think they are coordinating their respective behaviors. Whatever the answer, they are already prepared to consider the notion of communicative situations as either a denotative or an instructional and interactive conception of language and communication and to reach their own conclusions by analyzing the communicative situations in which García Márquez's grandfather supposedly narrated his story and the narrative situation in which García Márquez felt the need to imitate him. What does it mean to say that García Márquez chose to narrate as his grandfather did while knowing that the two communicative situations were vastly different? And what are the differences? His grandfather's narrative was oral and alien to the context of literary practices and norms, but *One Hundred Years* was written and clearly inscribed in a complex literary tradition for a different audience.

One Hundred Years, like any other novel, is understandable as not only the series of narrated events and the descriptions of the characters participating in them but also the norms to which the novel conforms or from which the text departs. Thus, to narrate as his grandfather did can be understood from two different perspectives. On the one hand, the novelist creates a narrative situation in which the narrator pays attention to common sense and causal law but adopts a worldview in which the narrated events that are beyond causal laws are narrated as if they were natural. On the other hand, the novelist creates a narrator who is writing a narrative in the same style that his grandfather used to tell stories orally.

Once the differences between oral and written narratives have been properly framed, the students are invited to turn their attention to the differences between the narrative situation in *One Hundred Years* and the narrative situation in less innovative novels. By the time we discuss *One Hundred Years*, the students have already read at least one late nineteenth- or early twentieth-century novel. Once they are able to analyze communication as semiotic interactions in a consensual domain and not just as the transmission of information or as the author's intended meaning, the students can compare oral and nonliterary with written and literary communicative situations, as well as literary communicative situations from different times. Furthermore, they are able to distinguish between the real communicative situation in which the author is interacting with an audience from the fictional communicative situation in which a narrator interacts with a fictional audience. This experiment allows the students to reflect on the universal function of narrative (using García Márquez's grandfather as an example) contrasted with the more restricted and regional function of literary narratives called novels.

At this point everybody's question is, "Under what conditions does a narrative become a novel?" The textual status of Melquíades's parchments becomes our basis of discussion. I ask the students to recount the plot without referring to the book or checking for information they did not remember well and to mention briefly what kind of difficulties, if any, they encountered in summarizing the plot. Here is one student's recounting:

> The plot of *One Hundred Years of Solitude* is that of a family's history spread over one hundred years. Maybe there is an underlying message in the book, but the point is made through the writing of the Gypsy Melquíades. At the end, when Aureliano finally transcribes the writings, he finds a thought which says the first of the generation shall be tied to a tree and the last shall be eaten by ants. Without going too deep into the meanings of everything, the book just describes different generations of a family, their similarities (especially those who carry the same first name) and their need to return to Macondo because they could really only exist with members of their own family. The last line sums up the whole book: ". . . races condemned to one hundred years of solitude did not have a second opportunity on earth." The loneliness and ineptitude of each member causes the end of the family tree. I did not have a problem coming up with this plot, because I see it plainly throughout the book. I may be only looking at the surface, but that is what I see.

The students seldom include Melquíades's parchments as a part of the novel. When asked why they considered only the Buendía family as the main actors of the plots and why they didn't include the writing and the deciphering of the Melquíades parchments as possible "actor" candidates, their answers are usually like the one suggested in the above summary: "the point is made through the writing of the Gypsy Melquíades." In other words, the plot is perceived through Melquíades's manuscripts, but Melquíades himself, his writing of the parchments, and the attempts of the Buendía family members to understand them is not considered part of the plot. When I suggested that at the end of the novel the emphasis is on the act of reading and writing, the students began to realize that the "actors" were not only the members of the Buendía family and Melquíades but also Melquíades's writing of the history of the family and Aureliano's attempting to decipher (read) it. To make the suggestion understandable and acceptable, I describe some of the literary norms and conventions the novel is alluding to—for example, the modern concept of writing (*écriture*), reading and writing as two fundamental operations in a modern concept of literature, the *mise en abime*, the idea of postmodernity, and the writings of Borges, Calvino, and Beckett—and show how they work when applied to understanding reading and writing processes.

The novel, we must remember, belongs to a specific historical, social, and cultural context. The trap of cultural arrogance, whereby the novel is remade into a world that is exotic and colorful, can be avoided if we reflect on the fact that the work was written by someone in a concrete human context and that all readers are also in their own concrete human contexts. With these ideas in mind, we approach literature as a complex system of interactions governed by conventions of writing and norms of reading.

García Márquez's Nobel Prize address is a useful introduction to the issue, specifically, the following quotation:

> To interpret our reality through schemas which are alien to us only has the effect of making us even more unknown, even less free, even more solitary. Perhaps venerable old Europe would be more sympathetic if it tried to see us in its own past; if it remembered that London needed three hundred years to build her first defensive wall and another three hundred before her first bishop. . . . Even in the culminating phase of the Renaissance, twelve thousand mercenary lansquenets of the Imperial armies sacked and razed Rome, cutting down eight thousand of its inhabitants.   ("Solitude of Latin America" 211)

The traditional incompatibility between European perspectives and Latin American reality opens the discussion of cross-cultural understanding. Further discussion of this issue comes later in the course, with a comparison between García Márquez's view of Latin America and Rigoberta Menchú's experiences of a Quiché community. I ask the students to think, on the one hand, about how García Márquez describes the cross-cultural relations between Europe and Latin America and, on the other hand, about the angle from which Rigoberta Menchú considers the opposition between her own Quiché culture and the Spanish tradition. This comparison allows me to emphasize the multilingual and pluricultural character of the Latin American culture.

From Narrative to (Latin American) Novels is the title under which I teach advanced students Latin American narrative of the twentieth century, including *One Hundred Years*. Although I do not always include the same texts, the criteria remain the same. During the semester the students read a sample of texts ranging chronologically from the end of the nineteenth century to the present and stylistically from naturalist and modernist narratives to challenging contemporary novels (such as *Casa de campo* by José Donoso and *Respiración artificial* by Ricardo Piglia) and direct testimonial narratives (*Biografía de un cimarrón* by Miguel Barnet and *Me llamo Rigoberta Menchú y asi nació mi conciencia* by Rigoberta Menchú). These books offer a way in which *One Hundred Years* can be contrasted and better understood. Students with a comparative bent are free to include non-Spanish-language contemporary narratives in their oral presentations and final papers.

Some of the questions I submit to the students at the beginning of the course are similar to the questions I raise in my literature-in-translation course. Others are new and specific to this level, such as questions about the nature of narratives, in which I probe into the distinction between their oral and written manifestations. We discuss theoretical works by Paul Ricoeur ("Model of the Text") and by Katharine Galloway Young, among others. This exercise pays off when the students have to compare, for example, the narrative situation in *One Hundred Years* with the one in Barnet's *Biografía de un cimarrón* or Menchú's *Me llamo Rigoberta Menchú*. We depart from the idea that a third-person, omniscient narrative voice, which García Márquez predominantly exploits, is the most elaborate mode of writing narrative. The narrative situation can be almost completely erased in third-person, omniscient narratives; but in oral communication the physical dimension of the situation (the narrator is there, in front of the audience) can be neither avoided nor forgotten. Between these two extremes of the spectrum, some of the testimonial narratives (especially *Biografía de un cimarrón* and *Me llamo Rigoberta Menchú*) are interesting cases in which previous oral communicative situations (the cimarrón telling the story to Barnet or Rigoberta Menchú telling the story to Burgos-Debray) are embedded in another communicative situation in which Barnet and Burgos-Debray transform the oral narrative into a written narrative of a different genre. The detailed analyses of oral narratives in their different aspects developed by Galloway Young, for example, are useful in examining their basic components and working out the paths that go from oral to written narratives, from written narratives to novels, and from novels to novels of a specific linguistic and cultural tradition, Spanish or Latin American in this case.

Before dealing with the problems of the cultural area, we have to face the transformation of a narrative into a novel. Topical courses are cumulative; we may devote two weeks to the discussion of *One Hundred Years*, but we do not lose sight of the novel afterward, for it is constantly being referred to and compared with other novels to elaborate on various aspects of the proposed topic. In this course I further develop the theory of the novel. I ask my students to summarize and compare three descriptions or definitions of the novel: the one expressed by writers themselves (students read essays by and interviews with García Márquez, especially the interview with Mario Vargas Llosa immediately after the publication of *One Hundred Years* [García

Márquez and Vargas Llosa]); the idea of the novel described by José Ortega y Gasset from a phenomenological orientation; and Mikhail Bakhtin's viewpoint as a literary theoretician ("Discourse in the Novel"). These three perspectives allow the students to elaborate further the transition from narrative to novels. García Márquez's conception of the novel and his idea of its function in society authorize the students to understand the similarities and the differences between writers' social roles in modern societies and storytellers' social roles in traditional societies—for example, García Márquez's grandfather's role. The approaches of Ortega y Gasset and Bakhtin allow the students to compare theories of narrative (Galloway Young) with theories of the novel and to apply theories of the novel to answer questions about the transitions from the narrative to the novel. I ask my students to think about how each theory considers the essential aspects in different novels and how helpful or limited these approaches are in accounting for the problems posed by novels such as *One Hundred Years* and narratives such as *Me llamo Rigoberta Menchú* and *Biografía de un cimarrón*. Ortega y Gasset helps the students find similarities between *One Hundred Years* and some of the nineteenth-century novels Ortega y Gasset refers to; Bakhtin gives them the means to identify differences and to grasp the function of narrative events, such as the writing and the reading of Melquíades's parchments. Neither Ortega y Gasset nor Bakhtin helps much in understanding *Biografía* and *Me llamo Rigoberta Menchú*, but Galloway Young does. At this point the students have enough material to prepare an oral presentation or a written report about the transition from oral narratives to novels and back to oral-written narratives. The students are able to place *One Hundred Years* in this spectrum as a novel in which traditional novelistic narrative modes have been kept and transformed according to current literary styles. García Márquez's statement that he decided to narrate *One Hundred Years* the way his grandfather used to tell stories to his friends acquires a new and more complex meaning (Fernández-Braso, *La soledad*).

Under what conditions is a narrative, such as *One Hundred Years*, not just a novel but a Latin American novel? By now the students are already familiar with the notion of context of description or interpretation. This notion, introduced at the beginning of the course, means that to understand something (an object, an event, a sentence, a text), you need a context in which the object or text acquires its meaning. A common context of description is the so-called historical, which is not existing but created by the interpreter. Other contexts of descriptions that we use are narrative, literature, and novel. Latin American novel is a fourth context that includes the previous ones. But these instructions are not enough to help the students answer questions such as the ones I have in mind: Under what conditions is a novel considered within a linguistic, cultural, and literary tradition? Does something in the novel or in the reader's mind or in both establish the connections between the novel and a linguistic, cultural, or literary tradition? Why, for example, do we ask questions about the place of *One Hundred Years* in the context of the Latin American novel and not, instead, in the context of the Colombian novel or in the context of the novel in the Western tradition? The answers to these questions are promptly articulated: it is our (as a class) or my (as the instructor) decision to select such and such a context of descriptions, instead of alternative ones. The root of the decision goes beyond the classroom and the instructor and touches on the curriculum and the accepted conventions, according to which literature in a Spanish program is taught in the context of the Spanish tradition and not, for example, in the context of comparative literature (for which established departments or programs can include Latin American literature) or in the context of literary theory (for which English and comparative literature departments have developed courses of study). A new dimension is added to our course: we talk about what the students are learning, the place of this course in the curriculum, the communicative situation in which we are engaging when talking about communicative situations.

When dealing with the inscription of a novel in a given context (Latin American novel and Latin American literature), we need a historical context of description, how the text requires the reader to create a context. Consequently, the students are encouraged to think about such issues as these: What kind of information in *One Hundred Years* points toward a given conception of Latin American history and culture? What are the functions of literature and the novel in society for García Márquez and for other writers?

In relation to the first question, the students are introduced to concepts and principles with which they can analyze the differences between historiographic and literary narratives; between conventions of truthfulness (for example, what we say when we expect our listeners to assume that what we say is true, regardless of whether it is really the truth by whatever measures we use to assess the truth of a statement) and conventions of fictionality (for example, what we say when we expect our listeners to understand that it is a game of make-believe) (Mignolo, "Dominios borrosos"). Once these distinctions are elaborated, I expose the students to other contemporary novels in which the authors assume the function of historians and decide to narrate important moments, periods, or events of Latin American history (Mignolo, "Ficcionalización," 209–10; *Teoría del texto*, 231–72). I invite the students to ponder why a writer in Latin America is compelled to take over the task of the historian, whether to narrate specific events of modern and contemporary history (dictatorship novels), of the colonial period, or an overview of the general history of Latin America, as is the case in *One Hundred Years*. Answers to these questions do not come easily, since they require a knowledge of Latin American history that undergraduate students do not usually have.

Aspects other than the rewriting of Latin American history help in placing a novel such as *One Hundred Years* in a given tradition. I give some consideration to the concept of magical realism, with which the novel is often affiliated (Mignolo, *Teoría del texto* 113–60), at two levels: at a semantic and referential level we examine the logico-semantic structure of narratives in which nonnatural events occur and at a historic and literary level we negotiate the relation between such events, their role in literary history, and their significance within a cultural tradition. A basic distinction between actual and possible worlds allows the students to deal with events that are acceptable to our common sense and those that, although taking place in a narrative world, are nonnatural according to our everyday standards. *One Hundred Years* and García Márquez's short stories offer plenty of opportunities to fill and organize index cards with nonnatural events, whether they are impossible events (human beings flying) made possible (a character in the García Márquez short story "Un señor" has wings) or possible events whose numerical dimension makes them extraordinary.

Once the students have grasped the logic of nonnatural or extraordinary events, we move to the level of deciding when an event can be considered an example of fantastic or magical realistic literature. I ask the students who should be in a position to make such a decision. We let the writers do the talking and read Alejo Carpentier ("Prólogo") and Miguel Angel Asturias ("Introducción a la novela") about magical realism and Guy de Maupassant and Jorge Luis Borges about the fantastic. After these readings we return to the logico-semantic structures of nonnatural narrative events in the context of both literary traditions, the fantastic and the magical realistic. Whatever position the students have taken vis-à-vis the topic, they have to confront the fact that the nature of a narrative event does not tell us about its fantastic or magical realistic properties. The characterization seems to be a combination of the event's logico-semantic structure and a context of description in which it can be understood and described. García Márquez's Nobel Prize address ("Solitude of Latin America") is a useful point of reference. In this short but dense lecture, García Márquez traces the history of Latin America from the perspective of his literary perception. He found in early writers, such as Antonio Pigafetta and Alvar Nuñez Cabeza de Vaca, the adventure "into the imagination" and "the madness of history" that allows him to conclude:

> I dare to believe that it is this highly unusual state of affairs, and not only its literary expression, which, this year, has merited the attention of the Swedish Literary academy: a reality which is not one on paper but which lives in us and determines each moment of our countless daily deaths, one which constantly replenishes an insatiable fount of creation, full of unhappiness and beauty, of which this wandering and nostalgic Colombian is merely another number singled out by fate. (209)

At this point the students have enough evidence to draw their own conclusions about the meaning of magical realism, its difference from fantastic literature, and its significance in a literary tradition that García Márquez creates by rewriting the history of Latin America.

Throughout the course the discussion of communication and understanding across cultural boundaries grows as each novel is read. García Márquez's contributions to this topic emerge from the continuation of his Nobel Prize address:

> For, if these setbacks benumb us, we who are of its essence, it is not difficult to understand that the mental talents of this side of the world, in an ecstasy of contemplation of their own culture, have found themselves without a proper means to interpret us. One realizes this when they insist on measuring us with the same yardstick with which they measure themselves, without recalling that the ravages of life are not the same for all, and that the search for *one's own identity is as arduous and as bloody for us as it was for them.* To interpret our reality through schemas which are alien to us only has the effect of making us even more unknown, even less free, even more solitary. (210; emphasis added)

I make use of this paragraph to emphasize that we may communicate with people from other cultures without necessarily reaching an understanding. Learning a language is a necessary step but not the sole condition for understanding people from a culture different from our own. Awareness of cross-cultural differences and the procedures to make a conscientious effort to understand should be one of the main goals of undergraduate foreign language and literature departments. The procedure for achieving these goals depends on the formation and the experience of the teacher. I begin with a summary and a simplification of an important but difficult article by Juri Lotman. He conceives of a human culture as a self-organized system in which those who belong and participate are, at the same time, those in charge of conceptualizing and regulating the system of which they are a part. Lotman calls *metalanguage* the conceptualization by which the members of a given culture conceive themselves as a unity in space and time with boundaries dividing *we* from *they*, *us* from *others*, *inside* from *outside*, *center* from *periphery*. Next, I ask the students to complement Lotman's proposal with Clifford Geertz's notion of looking at cultures "from the native point of view." I then ask the students to analyze the underlying conception of Latin American identity in García Márquez's novel and in his Nobel Prize address, as an example of a culture's metalanguage, and to compare both with the sense of identity emerging from Rigoberta Menchú's narrative, as an example of a different culture's metalanguage. I emphasize that the idea of Latin America expressed in García Márquez's writings may not be shared by the entire population of a multilingual and pluricultural continent. For example, Rigoberta Menchú writes of her community:

> There are twenty-two indigenous ethnic groups in Guatemala, twenty-three including the *mestizos*, or *ladinos*, as we call them. Twenty-three groups and twenty-three languages. I belong to one of them—the Quiché people—and I practise Quiché customs.   (1–2)

This statement helps us understand that to be a Quiché is something different from being a Latin American, even if those who identify themselves respectively as Quiché and Latin American share the geographical space called Latin America. The course is successful if the students understand that, while we cannot detach ourselves from our own culture and tradition, we should become critical observers by comparing our culture with others, instead of measuring what we don't know with the yardstick of what we do know. I let the students know that, although I agree with what García Márquez has to say about the European view of Latin America, I also believe that this agreement should be critically examined, as the example of Rigoberta Menchú forces us to do. I am convinced that promoting this kind of critical reflection is an important task for departments of foreign languages and literature.[1]

NOTE

[1]The position I take in this paper regarding undergraduate education owes a great deal to the discussions on critical thinking and the undergraduate curriculum started at the University of Michigan in 1984. I am especially thankful to Jack Meiland (philosophy department), Larry Mohr (political science department), and the University of Michigan Collegiate Fellows (1986–88) for discussions about innovations in the curriculum at the undergraduate level.

INTERPRETIVE APPROACHES FOR THE CLASSROOM

An Approach Using Ideology and History

Gabriela Mora

Like other often-used terms, *ideology* has many definitions, and disputes about its meaning have continued since Marxist theorists made it a key concept for understanding social formations. Equating ideology with false consciousness and setting it in opposition to scientific truth is no longer accepted, but the power of ideologies to influence human phenomena, including the sciences, is widely recognized. Gayatri Chakravorty Spivak considers ideologies "loosely articulated sets of historically determined and determining notions, presuppositions and practices" taken as "self-evident truth" (97). John B. Thompson asserts that the theory of ideology seeks "to examine the ways in which 'meaning' or 'ideas' affect the conceptions or activities of the individuals and groups" (73). Central to the organization of experiences and the construction of the subject, entities like the family, the church, the school, the judicial system, unions, and mass media—all part of Louis Althusser's ideological state apparatus—contribute to the creation of those notions, practices, meanings, and ideas. People use ideologies, consciously or unconsciously, to explain themselves and the world, and ideologies are linked to questions of power and domination, as Thompson emphasizes throughout his work.

Recognition of the ideological character of cultural phenomena has been reinforced by the current flourishing of semiotics. The category of the reader, accepted as an indispensable component in the production of the text, makes it impossible to obliterate the fact that we all bring our particular preconceptions to reading. Writers and critics, who are also the products of specific historical and social formations, inevitably infuse their work with their ideological views, which color the interpretations they create. Some critics see *One Hundred Years of Solitude*, for example, as entertainment posing no serious questions (Griffin); others read it as a kind of socialist history of Latin America (Martin). Some see the novel as a development of esoteric principles of alchemy (Halka, *Melquíades*). Others view *One Hundred Years* as "reality called fiction" because the author closely follows Colombian history (Mercado Cardona).

Since it is difficult to speak about ideologies without considering their historical contexts, some knowledge of Latin American and Colombian history is indispensable for analyzing and teaching *One Hundred Years*. Lucila Inés Mena, Stephen Minta, and Homero Mercado Cardona, among other critics, have traced the historical events that are woven into the fictional material. At this juncture it suffices to note the general historical phenomena crucial for interpreting the novel. These include colonialism, neocolonialism, and imperialism, which have plagued Latin America since its "discovery." Discussion of colonial rule and United States intervention through the Monroe Doctrine, the Platt amendment, and the creation of Panama, among other events, can provide students with a historical framework for examining some of the questions the book poses. The writings of Tulio Halperín Donghi and Eduardo Galeano are helpful here.

Gabriel García Márquez has said that his ideological premises are based on Marxist principles, a statement supported by some of the novel's features. For teachers to become familiar with those principles, Fredric Jameson (*Marxism and Form*), Terry Eagleton, and Catherine Belsey offer good introductions to the complex development of Marxian studies. Belsey's *Critical Practice*, in particular, presents a clear account of the seminal works of Louis Althusser and Pierre Macherey and helps the instructor think of *One Hundred Years* as a narrative constructed in opposition to classic realism, a mode Belsey explains in detail. By revising some linguistic (Benveniste) and psychological (Lacan) premises, Belsey allows us to see ideology as "inscribed in signifying practices as discourse and myth" (42).

One Hundred Years attempts to encompass human existence in its totality (McMurray, *García Márquez*), and the explication of this totality confronts the critic who wishes to read the ideologies in such a rich novel. Lack of class time makes it advisable to focus on those points that are crucial for bringing the students closer to the "total message" of the book. This message is directly related to the ending of the novel, in which the Buendía family is destroyed and, with them, Macondo, the town they helped create. The elucidation of this final episode is the key to understanding many textual enigmas, and its reading reveals the critic's ideology. For Gerald Martin, the Buendías' destruction means the end of an era dominated by European and United States imperialism in Latin America. Víctor Farías sees the disappearance of the Buendías as the logical outcome of a historical phase in which upper-class families have been unable to make a history different from that narrated in the novel. Farías, basing his reading on García Márquez's statement that *solitude* is the opposite of *solidarity*, agrees with Martin in ascribing the end of the Buendías to their fixation on themselves. Unable to reach out and love others, they yield to incest, which, like solitude, can be understood politically as a metaphor of the family's selfish egotism. Rejection of self-centeredness also accords with the novel's "collective subject of enunciated and enunciation," proposed by Tzvetan Todorov ("Macondo"). Todorov argues that the narrator places himself in the world he is depicting, adopting the views of the characters and the audience. Such a focus explains in part the novel's oral quality of discourse, the plurality of perspectives, and the perplexing mixture of the real and the imaginary.

But why do the Buendías represent antisolidarity, and why do they embody so many negatives, as Anna Marie Taylor, Gerald Martin, and others have suggested? With the notable exception of Víctor Farías, few have answered these questions and then only partially. Arguing that *One Hundred Years* was written from a "historical and class perspective" (19), Farías reads the novel as a meditation on how Latin America's possibilities were thwarted by the national bourgeoisie—represented by the Buendías—who sold out their countries to foreign interests and created class societies that are antisolidarian.

Today Marxists question the simplistic ("reductive") meaning that their predecessors attributed to class, and they debate its place among major determinants of ideologies (Connell; Laclau). But in the 1950s and 1960s when García Márquez was thinking about his book, class, essentially linked to economics, was the foundation on which the left built its analysis of Latin America's history. Since clear discursive traces in *One Hundred Years* expose the Buendías' class status and provide a useful hermeneutical guide, as Farías and other critics have shown, I use it to explain some of the novel's principal events and characters, illustrating their ideological aspects. Critical here is the demonstration of the Buendías' membership in the dominant class and their consciousness of their actions. This awareness of their knowledge of the choices open to them is significant for clarifying the problem of determinism in the portrayal of the family.

The beginning and the end of the Buendía story are marked by two historical events that can be thought of as the external factors in the family's demise: the flight of their ancestors from the pirate Drake and the final decline of Macondo, caused by the North American banana company. The town's birth and death, initiated by two foreign forces, underline the crucial role of imperialism in Latin America and reveal the correlation of the fictional with the historical in the novel. Macondo's fate reflects Latin America's colonial and neocolonial trajectory, as Mena and Mercado Cardona, among others, have illustrated.

García Márquez chose, however, to concentrate on the internal causes of Macondo's destruction, and here it is important to understand what the Buendías represent. To begin with, they constitute a lineage, an ideologically rich term that the narrator frequently uses when referring to the family. *Linaje*, besides its biological meaning, has the ideological nuance of power. Students are helped by a brief discussion of the significance of class divisions in Spain before and after the conquest of America and the specific connotations of words such as *linaje* and *casta*. Teachers should be aware that the meaning is lost in the English translation of *linaje* as "line" or, even worse, "race." The same happens with *casta* and *descastado*, because the sense of a privileged or special group is missing in the translation (139; 161).

The Buendías' ancestry confirms their membership in the upper class. Ursula is a descendant of Spaniards, and her husband comes from a family of tobacco planters. The European origin, a sign of an illustrious lineage in Latin America, and the fortune from the Iguarán-Buendía business partnership undoubtedly place the family in the upper echelon. Ursula and José Arcadio left their hometown already formed by cultural traits (ideologies), most of which derive from their social status. The money Ursula inherited and the fact that she and her husband are literate give them prominence among the first settlers.

Ursula, seen by most readers as the backbone of the family, shows characteristics that resonate with class ideology. When she invites only the descendants of the town's founders to celebrate the opening of the Buendía home, the narrator comments that it was "truly a high-class list," excluding even the newly arrived Moscotes (59; 65). As was the custom among the upper classes, Ursula furnished her house, the best in Macondo, with European luxuries. Although the Buendías are prominent Liberals, noted for their anticlericalism, Ursula dreams of having her great-grandchild become pope. Her emphasis on religion contributes to the miseducation of the two last male Buendías.

Class ideology is also present in the Buendías' founding of Macondo after their crime of honor, an offense usually associated in Spanish literature and culture with aristocracies. When critics write about the paradisiacal quality of the town's first years, they do not mention Macondo's origin in murder. It is not difficult to find more clouds in this "paradise," such as José Arcadio's neglect of his family and community while he pursues illusory projects. Moraima Semprún Donahue deals with other problems of the paradise when she studies gold and yellow as symbols in the novel. Like Farías, she sees a dialectic of progress and decadence in the Buendías' actions that eventually lead them to destruction. Clearly, Macondo was not born without a history or outside historical time, as some critics claim (Jara and Mejía Duque).

In the second generation of the Buendías, Aureliano, the colonel, best represents the contradictions and the frustrated possibilities that the family embodies. According to the narrator, the war gives Aureliano a chance to peep into "the abyss of greatness" (145; 158). This paradoxical uniting of low and high epitomizes the complicated manner in which vices and virtues compound Aureliano's profile. He possesses courage, a sense of justice, and qualities of leadership. But he has a barren heart, more prone to rage than to love, with pride fueling most of his actions.

Of the various opportunities Aureliano has to change the course of events, such as when he commutes the death sentence of his friend Gerineldo, his capitulation and signing of the Neerlandia Treaty (a real Colombian agreement) is crucial. Aureliano put down with great cruelty a rebellion of the officers who resisted "the selling of their victory" (the English translation omits this important phrase [149; 164]). When money for the revolution appears just at the moment he is about to sign what amounts to a betrayal of his principles, Aureliano misses the last opportunity to win the war. Later, Aureliano realizes what he did and bitterly ponders whether he could have changed his destiny at that moment (206; 224).

Along with an inability to love, Aureliano shows another revealing trait: he is the only member of the family unable to see Melquíades's magical room as spotlessly untouched by time. Since he is described as a lucid man with the faculty of prediction, his blindness to magic can be read as the ability to perceive better than others the truth about his family and his environment. If this is so, the fact that he cannot see his father's ghost and urinates on him and the ancestral tree may be interpreted as contempt for himself and his family. Even if this reading is contested, the irreverence toward family founders and their lineage is clear.

The Buendía family helped create the *latifundio*, an institution closely linked with the upper classes. Teachers interested in reading *One Hundred Years* as a document illustrating Latin American historical reality can discuss how the *latifundio*—which, together with the church and the government, forms the classical trinity blamed for Latin American ills—is the offspring of violence and theft. In the novel, José Arcadio, the founders' older son, terrorizes the peasants with his dogs and his shotgun, despoiling them of their best plots of land. His son, Arcadio, becomes "the cruelest ruler that Macondo had ever known" (95; 105), using his position in the Liberal government to legalize the ownership of the stolen lands and to embezzle Macondo's taxes to build a house in the heart of the town. Later, the land seizures are recognized as legal by the Conservatives, showing the complicity between the two parties, a historical fact in Colombia (Mercado Cardona).

Instrumental in consolidating the power of the church, the Buendías invite the first priest to Macondo to celebrate the union of Aureliano, the future colonel, with Remedios Moscote. This marriage formalizes the integration of class and government and marks the penetration of force into Macondo, for Moscote comes as a magistrate and brings armed guards with him. The resulting society is one in which schools "accepted only the legitimate offspring of Catholic marriages" (289; 314), a rule that even denies an education to the last Buendía, born out of wedlock.

Aureliano Segundo's choice to marry Fernanda del Carpio increases the power of social and religious prejudice. As a representative of the most retrograde form of aristocracy and as a factor in the fall of the Buendía family, Fernanda offers ample possibilities for ideological analysis. Students can search for discursive signs suggesting that she is portrayed more as a carrier of death than as a giver of life (for example, the funeral wreaths she makes and her plan to kill her grandchild). The heavy, satirical strokes with which this character is depicted call to mind the portraits of those Spanish *hidalgos* from classic literature who had the same blind pride and the same empty coffers. Besides this intertextual connection, the government's involvement in Fernanda's plot to get rid of Babilonia, whose only crime was his plebeian origin, must be stressed. Social prejudices ruin the future of Fernanda's daughter and cripple her grandchild's development.

Macondo's emergence as a town governed by powerful families, the church, and the army represents Colombia's history through the nineteenth century, as Mena (*La función*), Janes (*García Márquez*) and Minta have shown. The intertwined fictions and historical events of the latter part of *One Hundred Years* belong to the twentieth century, when the banana company was established. Macondo's dependence on foreign capital is analogous to the well-documented situation of many Latin American countries (Galeano; Halperín Donghi). In the novel, the company commands the power and the resources previously reserved to divine Providence. Social customs and the courses of rivers are changed by the foreign owners, who later cause the deluge that almost destroys the town. The text makes clear that the company's policies create the undernourished women whom Fernanda and Meme do not see when riding the train to the convent, where pregnant Meme is to be confined forever (250–73).

Students should be made aware that in *One Hundred Years* the central government and the class represented by the Buendías open the way for the banana company. A colonel's son brings the railroad that helps establish the banana business, and Aureliano Segundo welcomes Mr. Herbert to his home and introduces him to the fruit. Both actions are a clear reminder of the historical collusion of the high bourgeoisie and foreign interests. Ursula, as well as Aureliano Segundo, delights in the "progress" brought by the Americans, and the family reaches the zenith of its prosperity during the company's reign. Aureliano Segundo's mindless and continuous revel, which the narrator calls the "apotheosis of squandering" (167; 184), mirrors similar behavior of the Latin American rich. The mysterious proliferation of Aureliano Segundo's animals, associated with his love for Petra Cotes, may be an ironic metaphor alluding to the inexplicable origins of many great fortunes. Ursula calls him *"un cuatrero"* ("cattle rustler") (167; 183), suggesting one source of Aureliano Segundo's wealth, while his nickname, "Mr. Providence," given him by the Macondians, is another discursive analogy tying him to the company. Aureliano Segundo spends the last of his money to send his children to study in Europe, as the Latin American upper classes did in the nineteenth century.

José Arcadio Segundo, who works as the company's foreman, also deserves special attention. The narrator of *One Hundred Years* repeatedly comments on José Arcadio Segundo's feeling of estrangement from the Buendías, even claiming that he "was not a member of the family" (225; 245). This syntagma may be a reminder of José Arcadio Segundo's unusual break with family tradition when he goes to work for the Americans and later becomes a leader of the workers. But he does belong to the family, as is proved, first, by his failure in different enterprises; then as a labor leader unable to prevent the massacre; and, above all, by the way he spends his last years. When he hides in Melquíades's room, obsessively reading the gypsy's manuscript, he is the colonel's homologue in defeat and withdrawal from society.

In writing about the massacre of the workers, García Márquez closely follows the historical evidence, even using the actual names of some of the participants (Mena, *La función*; Mercado Cardona). It is important for the teacher to dwell on this history and the significance of the villagers' loss of memory (Taylor). If fear is the cause of the Macondians' amnesia after the massacre, the government's immediate actions show clearly how the ideological (press) and repressive (army and police) apparatuses impose forgetfulness on those who ordinarily remember well.

The loss of memory is a recurrent motif in the novel; in discussing it, the teacher should bring the historical connections to the students' attention. When the first pest of forgetfulness afflicts Macondo, it is associated with the Buendías' Indian servants. This phenomenon signals the absence of the Indian heritage from the official histories, as Taylor and Farías have noted. The danger of forgetting the past is illustrated by the killing of the colonel's remaining living son when the last two male Buendías fail to recognize him as their relative and refuse him the sanctuary he requests.

Forgetfulness also highlights the novel's main structural features of repetition and circularity. Most critics see the repetition of names and events as originating in a cyclical conception of history, useful for explaining the universal myths of the book and the obsession with the circularity of time shown by Ursula and her husband. Taylor, following Marx's theory of history as an evolutionary process, was one of the first to deny the existence of cyclical time in the novel's design. She hypothesizes that Macondo's final destruction is the last point in a progressive disintegration in which the lack of historical consciousness is a principal factor. The decline of the Buendías is confirmed by their final disappearance and by the observation of the longest-lived Macondian, Pilar Ternera: "the history of the family was a machine with unavoidable repetitions, a turning wheel that would have gone on spilling [sic] into eternity were it not for the progressive and irremediable wearing of the axle" (the Spanish reads *"dando vueltas"* 'spinning' [334; 364]).

The Buendías are the axle chosen by the author to represent the course of Macondo's history, and the portraits of the last male members clearly reveal the continuous wearing down as the family nears its end. José Arcadio, the would-be pope who greatly resembles his mother, Fernanda, is described as weak-lipped and languid (309; 336). Suffering from asthma, this self-centered man comes home only because of the inheritance his mother promised. The suggestion of his homosexuality is the maximum proof in this macho society of the weakening of a line so proud of its supermachos. By contrast, Aureliano Babilonia is more attractive, but he too fails to break the chain of his family's errors. He unites the intellectual and physical powers disassociated since the first pair of children, José Arcadio and Aureliano (a division with ideological implications), but cannot use them because it is too late, according to the book's conception of history. Although Aureliano Babilonia is the first to know friendship and love, he is unable to stop the family's destruction, because his "prolonged captivity, the uncertainty of the world," and "the habit of obedience had dried up the seeds of rebellion in his heart" (308; 336).

A better line of male Buendías could have been realized through the colonel's bastard sons, who grow up as peaceful, hardworking men, perhaps because of the influence of their humble mothers. Their abbreviated lives, however, are a consequence of the brutal fight between Conservatives and Liberals, to which the Buendía family contributed much.

As for the female characters, Amaranta is a true Buendía by virtue of her confused heart and deep sense of solitude. Amaranta, like Fernanda del Carpio, is a specialist in the rites of death and is conscious of her nefarious influence on many. She causes not only the death of her suitors but the unhappiness of several generations of her nephews. Amaranta's deathbed proclamation of virginity, after her recognition that she has left an "outpouring of misery" (237; 258), is a satirical finishing touch, mocking her rigid values and hypocrisy. Remedios the Beauty, contrary to Margaret Sayers Peden's view of her as a good woman and Farías's claim that she incarnates the spontaneity and the purity of the beginnings of the Buendía project, can be seen as another satirical portrait of a useless human being. Her lethal effect is confirmed by the death of four men. Because Remedios the Beauty is an idle, illiterate woman, "immune to any kind of passionate feelings" (190; 208), her ascension to heaven cannot be equated with the Virgin Mary, who represents care and love. Remedios's magical disappearance may be an ironic twist of the religious myth to underline the ideological premise that women like Remedios and Fernanda should not exist in worlds like Macondo, where violence and injustice require conduct different from theirs. The narrator seems to say this when he remarks that Remedios "was not a creature of this world" (188), and Fernanda "era mujer perdida para el mundo" (178). The English version, which reads "in the world," loses the meaning (195).

In contrast to the destructive Buendía women, the lower-class women are open and generous. Pilar, Santa Sofía de la Piedad, Petra, and Nigromanta (the last two are black) keep rescuing the inept and infantile men of the family from fear, poverty, and pain. Petra Cotes, for example, feeds the Buendías when they are on the verge of starvation and takes care of her rival, Fernanda, until her death. That the novel's punishments and rewards have specific ideological views of class, love, and race is shown by the escape from the final hecatomb of Santa Sofía de la Piedad, the Catalan bookdealer, and Gabriel the writer-narrator.

Love as practiced by the Buendías brings no happiness. The harmful division of intellect and instinct that the Aurelianos and the Arcadios represent is reflected in their separation of sexual passion and love. The Buendías are divided between the excessive fornicators and the sexually repressed. Both groups, however, long for a kind of love that they do not know or that they find too late. Aureliano Segundo and Petra are old when they discover the intense feeling of friendship that the narrator seems to value as a higher state of love. Amaranta Úrsula and the last Aureliano go from frenzied passion to the calm of real communication, but they also fall into the isolation damned by the book.

Melquíades and his magic room present the critic with another set of problems that a class approach does not completely explain. Answers to some of the enigmas about him can be found in the text. His resurrection is an example. The novel supports only one death of Melquíades, the one that occurred in Macondo, while the reports of his first death are only hearsay. His role as narrator of the story we read, on the other hand, is given by most critics to Gabriel, who went to Paris to write about Macondo (Mena, *La función*; Martin). Melquíades's manuscript, one must remember, disappears together with the town. Still, the question of why García Márquez chose to create a gypsy as a main character should be considered. Careful research on gypsies led Farías to see their presence in Macondo as a paradigm of free persons who, in contrast to the Buendías, do not own land and reject the state. Farías reminds us, however, that gypsies also embrace endogamy, superstition, and strict taboos. What makes Melquíades special is that he had the courage to break his tribe's laws. By learning more than was permitted, Melquíades transforms himself, becoming more universally human. Although he suffers expulsion by his people, he is Macondo's savior during the pest of forgetfulness, and he predicts a brighter future without the Buendía family. Melquíades is used in a historical and secular way, just as the author uses religious and other myths. The gypsy's room is but a metaphor, first representing a place where the Buendías have the possibility of knowing themselves and then a place of hiding, a locus of death and not life.

In discussing García Márquez's subtle blending of the imaginary and the real, we must note the use of hyperbole and humor, his celebrated trademarks. A good example is the case of the 1928 massacre that Colombian authorities denied took place (Mena, *La función*; Minta). In *One Hundred Years* the unreal quality of the nocturnal train snaking through the countryside and the cunning ways the company's lawyers manage to "prove" the nonexistence of the workers are metaphorical renderings of equally unbelievable but real historical events. The erasure and distortion of history, not an exclusive Latin American phenomenon, is the underlying subtext and confirms the fact that history, more often than not, is written from the seat of power.

Magical realism has been the confusing label most frequently used when referring to García Márquez's writing style (Rodríguez Monegal). Instructors may find Alejo Carpentier's reflections about his concept of *real maravilloso* more useful, especially his allusion to the existence in Latin America of geographical, social, and historical phenomena whose out of the ordinariness make them seem unreal to those who are not part of that world. The history of Latin America since its discovery is rich with accounts of the most extraordinary phenomena, as García Márquez pointed out in his Nobel prize acceptance speech ("Solitude of Latin America"). If learned men like Christopher Columbus, Antonio Pigafetta, and Alvar Nuñez Cabeza de Vaca could write about myth and consider it as real as the events they experienced, it is not surprising that the novelist narrates as real the Macondians' beliefs in ghosts and flying carpets.

Charming as some of these myths are, the merciless final annihilation of Macondo and the Buendías emphasizes the serious side of the Latin American reality. Some Marxist critics (Blanco Aguinaga; Rodríguez) object to the total destruction of Macondo in which even the workers disappear. But Macondo, like real present-day ghost towns, began to empty out soon after the disasters produced by the foreign company. With the agriculture ruined and industry closed, the workers left. The cyclonic wind at the end only finishes off what imperialism had begun, and this is what the novel underscores. As for García Márquez's "radical pessimism" supposedly confirmed by the book's end (Rodríguez-Luis), the annihilation of Macondo can be read otherwise. In cultivating their passions without concern for others, the Buendías built a city of "mirages" (351; 383). Failing to understand that solitude means alienation and a lack of solidarity with society, the family had to be destroyed. The pig's tail that marks the beginning and the end of the Buendías is thus an emblem of their blind egotism. The wise gypsy and Gabriel, the narrator, predict that "races condemned to one hundred years of solitude did not have a second opportunity on earth" because the world needs a better foundation (351; 383). Instead of pessimism, *One Hundred Years*'s ending stresses the author's ideologically based conviction that the Buendías will be replaced by others able to make history in a more just and humane way.

An Approach Using History, Myth, and Metafiction

Isabel Alvarez Borland

When asked by an interviewer to describe the essence of his novel, García Márquez replied, "*One Hundred Years of Solitude* is not a history of Latin America, it is a metaphor for Latin America" (Dreifus 74). The author's words affirm his awareness of having created a fiction that is simultaneously historical and mythical. In teaching *One Hundred Years*, I focus on the text's polarities so that students will think about the novel in its historical, mythical, and metafictional dimensions.

As history, the text functions as a metaphor for Latin America in which the perils of the Buendía family represent a scathing commentary on centuries of colonialism, civil war, and political chaos. As myth, the Buendía saga, with its juxtaposition of imagined and real events, speaks of the inadequacy of documentary history and the importance of oral history: the superstitions, dreams, and imaginations of the Macondians. As metafiction, Melquíades's manuscripts retell the story of the Buendía family as a tale meant to be reread and retold. The metaplot also allows students to reflect on the elusive boundaries that separate art from life and to question the uncertainties of their own reality. The jolting effect of the last chapter, with its awareness of the text as text, allows students to conceive of *One Hundred Years* as a work that simultaneously partakes in aesthetics, philosophy, and social consciousness.

I teach *One Hundred Years of Solitude* in the Department of Modern Languages at Holy Cross College as part of an advanced undergraduate offering in modern Spanish American narrative. The heterogeneity and the complexity of the novel demand an organized plan of what will be covered in class. Since I have only six class periods in which to discuss this text, I have to carefully choose the episodes and segments for discussion. After trying different approaches, I have decided that the best way to present this text to undergraduates is to devote each class to one chapter or segment that is representative of the specific topic considered. The topics discussed are announced in handouts ahead of time. Usually, two students present the chapter to be addressed in class, and then discussion is turned over to the rest of the group. In addition, students are assigned another segment or chapter that is not discussed in class to analyze on their own, relating the segment to the text's main social and aesthetic themes. I encourage the students to be creative in their approach, to base their papers on their own ideas, and to avoid repeating class notes unless the notes have a direct application to the chapter they have chosen.

Because our objective is to uncover the interaction between the historical, mythical, and metafictive aspects of the text, the teacher must do some preparatory reading. While the role of myth and history in *One Hundred Years* has been widely researched, the following articles are the basis of my approach to the teaching of the text: Carlos Fuentes's "García Márquez: La segunda lectura" in his *La nueva novela hispanoamericana* and Roberto González Echevarría's "*Cien años de soledad*: The Novel as Myth and Archive." Although written from different perspectives, both studies identify history, myth, and metafiction as central to the understanding of *One Hundred Years* and illuminate the polar tensions present in the novel. The books by Raymond L. Williams and Stephen Minta and the collection edited by Bernard McGuirk and Richard Cardwell provide useful background on García Márquez. In addition, I strongly suggest that teachers, as well as students, review the *New York Times* clippings of the year in which García Márquez won the Nobel prize (1982) and that they read at least one comprehensive interview with the author, such as Rita Guibert's interview in *Seven Voices*.

A general introduction to the concept of metafiction is Robert Alter's *Partial Magic* and Michel Foucault's essay on Velázquez's *Las Meninas*, which discusses metafiction from a visual perspective. Since the preceding three weeks of the course are spent studying metafictional stories by Jorge Luis Borges ("El aleph," "El tema del traidor y del héroe") and by Julio Cortázar ("La noche bocarriba," "Las babas del diablo"), the students are exposed to self-reflexive writing by the time they read *One Hundred Years*. During those first weeks, I bring in complementary visual works, such as M. C. Escher's *Drawing Hands*, Velázquez's *Las Meninas*, and Picasso's versions of Velázquez's *Meninas* to study the presence of the author in the text and the role of the intertext within the metafictive work. Finally, the dichotomy of history versus fiction is treated by Hayden White in "The Historical Text as Literary Artifact" in his *Tropics of Discourse* and by Mario Vargas Llosa in a brief article, "Is Fiction the Art of Lying?"

The following plan summarizes what is covered during the six periods allotted to the teaching of *One Hundred Years* (two class meetings a week).

Introduction

I begin by locating the novel in literary history and by referring to the literary conventions of the writers who, along with García Márquez, revolutionized Latin American prose during the 1960s (the so-called generation of the boom); it is in this context that *One Hundred Years* takes on its meaning. A useful introductory exercise is to read together "The Solitude of Latin America," García Márquez's 1982 Nobel Prize address. Next, as preparation for our approach to the novel, I ask my students to consider the differences between history and myth and to formulate their own definitions of both. Finally, we set out our reading goals for *One Hundred Years*. The students must follow the linear plot (the story of the town and of the family) and the metaplot (the writing and the eventual deciphering of the manuscripts by the various family members). By following the linear plot—which we divide into four main sections: the foundation, the war years, the American intervention, and Macondo's last days—the students become aware of the historical and the mythical aspects of the book and the difficulty of separating one dimension from the other. The novel's literary subtext is crucial to our interpretation and must be considered simultaneously with the linear plot. I ask the students to pay special attention to Melquíades and to the episodes about the translation of the manuscripts, since both have central roles in our aesthetic reading of the text. I advise the students to think of the novel as a text that questions itself and the reader by means of myth, history, and metafiction and to be aware that few answers are given to the questions posed by the narrative. In fact, García Márquez elicits reader responses through suggestion and challenge, not pontification. The students, as active participants in the process of reading, must formulate some answers. To further prepare the students, I show outside class *Gabriel García Márquez: La magia de lo real,* a documentary on how the Colombian region is recreated in the fictional world of *One Hundred Years.*

At the end of this first class, I hand out a list of chapters and the days on which they will be discussed. Since *One Hundred Years* is composed of twenty unnumbered segments, I usually ask the students to read four segments for each class, even if during our class time we limit ourselves to discussing only one segment in detail. Ideally, the students have read the entire book before we begin our discussion, and specific chapters are reread according to our reading plan.

Foundation of Macondo: Segments 1–4

This class's main objective is a thorough discussion of the novel's initial chapter; we study its process (artistic elaboration), as well as its product (the events that make up the story). We concentrate our analysis on García Márquez's treatment of some well-known biblical and classical myths. I remind the students that myths in García Márquez's text question the cultural identity of the Latin American and become a mirror of the society he depicts. However, García Márquez has written a novel in which no single myth or mythology prevails. By using both classical and biblical traditions, he has endowed his work with a mythical character. Finally, we review the role of myths as stories whose main concern is the discovery of origins, and we dwell on the universal quality of myths as they reveal aspects of human behavior and allow us to understand ourselves better.

We single out passages illustrating the biblical overtones in the description of Macondo's foundation and the role of incest and violence in the foundation of the town—that is, the story of Prudencio Aguilar. The gypsies, their inventions, and the relation between myth and imagination conclude this introduction to the text's mythical essence.

I remind the students that the mythical dimension in *One Hundred Years* is inseparable from the historical dimension and that for pedagogical purposes

I have chosen to isolate these essential components of the novel's fictional world. If time permits, a couple of enthusiastic students select their favorite passages from these initial segments and explain how the passages illustrate García Márquez's handling of a particular myth.

Macondo, Society, and the War Years: Segments 5–9

Just as the initial chapters provided a fine introduction to the book's mythical character, the next four segments are a transition to the historical chapters in the text. The fifth segment deals with García Márquez's relation to the institutions that shape Latin American society. In it García Márquez asks readers to question their beliefs about Macondo's institutions, the church and town government. We examine Father Nicanor Reyna, Apolinar Moscote, and Dr. Alirio Noguera in their symbolic roles as representatives of societal institutions. Finally, José Arcadio's ruling of Macondo during the war years can be used to discuss García Márquez's view of the futility of armed conflicts.

The advent of organized religion in Macondo is marked by the appearance of Father Nicanor Reyna. Seeing that the Macondians have no religion, Father Reyna decides to stay to spread what he thinks are Christian values. However, the reader learns that his main interest is the building of a cathedral, "the largest in the world, with life-size saints and stained-glass windows on the sides, so that people would come from Rome to honor God in the center of impiety" (85). Father Reyna's obsession with collecting money to build his church rounds off García Márquez's ironic portrait of organized faith and its goals.

Similarly, the arrival of Apolinar Moscote marks the beginning of politics and corruption in Macondo's local government. The residents fight with each other, and a bitter battle ensues between Liberals and Conservatives. Governments and politics are depicted as a fabrication made for the convenience of those in control. A confused Aureliano joins the Liberals, not really knowing what they stand for but knowing that he does not like the actions of the Conservatives. War is declared, and yet no one can define the causes of the conflict. Dr. Noguera, the town's doctor, is a further example of the deterioration of civic principles: his plans for the assassination of every Conservative family are his way of ending the evils of Conservatism.

Years of the American Intervention: Segments 10–15

Segments 10–15 lead to a discussion of García Márquez's relation to history. Can *One Hundred Years* be read as a historical account of Latin America during the years between 1850 and 1950? Can the text be divided into historical stages, with segments allotted to the years of the Spanish colonization, the wars of independence, the American intervention, and the present? I ask the students to reflect on the changes between the Macondo of the foundation years and the Macondo of the war years. Has there been any real progress?

To illustrate the basic heterogeneity of the novel, I contrast the goals of historical writing and mythical writing. If myth is equated with fiction—that is, with writing not concerned with a faithful depiction of reality—historical writing is its opposite, as the goals of the historian are to remain faithful to events as much as possible. If mythical writing is cyclical, historical writing strives to become a chronological, linear account of events. But I remind the students that both historical writing and mythical writing in *One Hundred Years* are inevitably concerned with the power of language and its misuse or misinterpretation.

Segment 15 shows the use of language to manipulate others into acquiescence at both the mythical level and the historical level. The chapter connects the historical wars of the previous section with the mythical decline of the final section, and it moves the novel toward its conclusion by introducing the last Aureliano and bringing the focus back to the parchments and to the novel's metafictional dimension. The segment can be divided into two parts: the mythical story of Meme and Mauricio Babilonia and the historical account of the great strike.

During the first part of this segment, Fernanda's response to Meme's affair; her mistreatment of her grandson, Aureliano Babilonia; and her correspondence with the "invisible doctors" show her manner of manipulating language in order to distort reality. In the second portion of the chapter, which describes the workers' massacre during the great strike, historical reality is either distorted or masked through language. The reader participates in the violent gathering with José Arcadio Segundo, rides out of Macondo, and arrives back in Macondo with him. After the massacre of several hundred people by government troops, José Arcadio Segundo encounters several distortions of reality similar to those created by Fernanda. When he seeks help, he is told: "There haven't been any dead here. . . . Since the time of your uncle, the colonel, nothing has happened in Macondo" (285). In addition, an official proclamation to the nation states that "the workers . . . had returned home in peaceful groups" (286). Finally, military officers state: "You must have been dreaming. . . . Nothing has happened in Macondo, nothing has ever happened, and nothing ever will happen. This is a happy town" (287).

Segment 15 demands a detailed stylistic analysis, for it contains rich, vivid metaphors of the crowd scenes during the shooting in Macondo. Moreover, the changing settings and the different styles of language in this segment allow students to experience the bewilderment of José Arcadio Segundo as a victim of the misuse of language.

If time permits, key episodes from segments 9–14—such as the ascension of Remedios the Beauty to heaven, the mythical powers of Petra Cotes, and the unusual aura of Mauricio Babilonia—can be analyzed to point out the relation between myth and the much-debated critical term magical realism.

Metafictional Chapters: Segments 16–20

The last five segments of the text bring it to a close and unfold the enigma of Melquíades's manuscripts. From the beginning, Melquíades is an enigmatic figure in the novel. His prophetic powers, his penchant for transmutations and transformations, and his passion for alchemy and its promise of immortality present a character at once mythical and literary.

This is a good time to review references to the manuscripts found in previous segments and to reconstruct the text's metafictional subtext. A review of the encounters of the Buendía family with Melquíades's manuscripts shows the importance of embedded readers and writers as crucial aspects of the book. The despotic Arcadio's first encounter with the manuscripts, Aureliano Segundo's futile attempts to decipher their code, and the eventual deciphering of the code by Aureliano Babilonia are all episodes that underscore the importance of reading and translation as forms of literary re-creation. As Robert Alter and others have stated, in reflexive fiction the reader must contemplate simultaneously the frame and what is represented inside the frame. Thus, metafiction implies a meditation on the nature of the medium in which the work presents itself. The students now know that they are immersed in the story or plot of *One Hundred Years* and are simultaneously aware of the power of this text as literature.

Because the events of the final segment are sweeping and powerful, I prepare the students for the novel's conclusion by analyzing the penultimate segment in detail. By this time the decay of the family and the town has reached a point where there is no turning back, the characters can no longer see reality, the process of involution through incest comes full circle. On her return to Macondo, Amaranta Ursula, sustained by her nostalgic view of the Macondo of earlier times, cannot see the decay prevalent in the house and in the town. Even though Aureliano causes the family to come to an end through his incestuous relationship with Amaranta Ursula he alone has the potential to reverse the long process of decay. In Melquíades's manuscripts, he holds the key to the future. If the manuscripts could be read— and Aureliano is close to deciphering them—the future would be known, and any potential wrongs could be averted. Aureliano knows the importance of the manuscripts, for he speaks to Amaranta Ursula of "the necessity of deciphering the predictions so that they would not defeat themselves" (360). The activity the manuscripts warned about, incest, caused him to turn away from the documents—in effect, eliminating the last possibility that could have saved the family.

Not knowing how to interpret reality's clues has been a constant throughout this text. As we indicated in segment 15, the government officials changed history when they denied that a massacre had ever taken place. They distorted reality, but later generations, brought up to believe these distortions, accepted them as truth (359). Similarly, Aureliano and Amaranta Ursula should have opened their eyes beyond their isolated existence to see the truth of their situation, but they were no more at fault than were Ursula and Jose Arcadio one hundred years earlier.

I ask the students to write a short paper in response to the events contained in the last segment of the text. Since the last chapter of *One Hundred Years* is an unsettling experience, these papers ensure the students' grappling with the text's reflexivity and encourage them to think about how metafiction relates to history and myth.

Conclusion

The sixth class is devoted to a close reading of the last pages of *One Hundred Years*, using as a point of departure the papers assigned in the previous class. We begin by briefly reviewing the final events: Amaranta Ursula dies after the birth of her child, Aureliano wanders in grief through the ruins of Macondo, the baby is eaten by the ants, and the manuscripts are finally deciphered. As Melquíades had announced to Aureliano Segundo, the manuscripts could be understood only when they had reached one hundred years. By now it is evident that the manuscripts contain the story of the family— that is, the novel itself. After seeing the remains of his child as "a dry and bloated bag of skin," Aureliano remembers the prophetic line: "The first of the line is tied to a tree and the last is being eaten by the ants" (381). It is now that Melquíades's code is revealed to Aureliano as he realizes that his own destiny is also found in the manuscripts: "Aureliano . . . began to decipher the instant that he was living, deciphering it as he lived it, prophesying himself in the act of deciphering the last page of the parchments, as if he were looking into a speaking mirror" (383).

The text's awareness of itself as literature becomes a key to the understanding of the mythic-historical essence of the novel. Metafiction forces readers into an awareness of writing and of the process of making a text as it simultaneously challenges them to an understanding of themselves. Seen in this manner, the metaplot synthesizes the seemingly opposite historic and mythical dimensions of the text.

Can *One Hundred Years* be at once a mythical novel and a historical novel? García Márquez tells us yes; in fact, only through these two dimensions can we apprehend the Latin American reality. Historical writing is a recording of the past and implies self-understanding through the remembering of that past. Myths, by contrast, allow self-understanding through the telling of tales that seek to explain who we are. The Buendía family's story is recorded for posterity as history but is cast in the language of myth and preserved as literature through the manuscripts of Melquíades. Melquíades's manuscripts become a lesson in how to read; many generations of the Buendía family do not know how to interpret his writings, their past, and thus are unable to gain control of their destinies.

In *One Hundred Years* metafiction challenges the reader to an understanding of the story of Latin America as it is told through myth and through the myths of history. The manuscripts as metafictive documents become a literary metaphor of what the mythical and the historical dimensions of the text have already told us: only in self-understanding can we meet the challenge of the Latin American predicament. Thus, Melquíades's manuscripts retell the story of the Buendía family as a story meant to be reread, examined, and retold. A metafictional reading of García Márquez's novel makes students better readers of literature in general and gives them an opportunity to see themselves in the mirror of Melquíades's manuscripts.

Archetypal Approaches

Robert L. Sims

Robert Scholes identifies three aspects of textual study: reading, interpretation, and criticism. He says that "each one of these can be defined by the textual activity it engenders. In *reading* we produce *text within text*; in *interpreting* we produce *text upon text*; and in criticizing we produce *text against text*." Scholes believes that the literature teacher's primary task consists in developing methods that enable students to "produce oral and written texts themselves in all three modes of textualization" (24). To accomplish these goals, the teacher must specify the textual level that a particular critical method addresses.

We can distinguish three textual levels that correspond to different critical approaches: pretextual, textual, and subtextual. The first level considers the text primarily as a reflection of the author's life and times or those of his characters. Modern textual criticism encompasses a broad range of approaches, including narratology, structuralism, semiotics, and deconstruction; these critical methods adopt an internal perspective and focus primarily on the structural components of the text. The subtextual level includes sociological and psychoanalytical approaches and archetypal and myth criticism—all of which view the text from an extrinsic perspective.

Preliminary Theoretical Considerations

As Eric Gould writes, "the archetypalist position is a very familiar one in literary studies, where it has sanctioned a long history of interpretation as the art of translating symbols into universal archetypes" (15). Archetypal criticism often focuses on areas that are not strictly textually based. Carl G. Jung is the most important figure in modern archetypal criticism, and his "belief that he has joined heaven and earth, the unconscious and the conscious, in the archetype is indeed what literary studies has found most interesting about his approach" (Gould 16). The purported link between mythology and literature that Jung establishes through archetypes enables him to provide an analytical framework that bridges the gap between multifaceted human experience and its expression in literature. Jung's theory of archetypes is useful because "it aims to objectify psychological processes, even while it satisfies our need to locate somewhere (however mysteriously) the universalizing function of symbols" (Gould 19). The problem raised by archetypalist interpretation is that it "is entirely dependent on the *arbitrary* emergence of those primordial image-symbols. We are in their grip, whether we like it or not, and yet we never really know what we are in the grip of" (Gould 21). In short, we are attempting to interpret what is not interpretable, and the archetype as a primordial image "simply dominates consciousness and gives birth to an art which lives in its shadows" (Gould 20).

The misapplication of archetypal criticism, therefore, runs the risk of

displacing or even replacing the text it purports to study. Discovering archetypes in literary texts can have a multiplier effect; characters, events,
and situations can be made to "fit" certain paradigmatic figures and patterns.
This can quickly induce students and teachers to superimpose an interpretive
framework that has little or nothing to do with the text. Archetypal criticism
demands an unlimited field of possibilities while its actual forms have a finite
and systematic nature. Archetypes provide ways of categorizing and essen-
tializing the human experience found in literature, and literary texts can be
reduced to catalogs of archetypal images. Archetypal approaches can also
lead students and teachers to "establish a system of reductive monism for
the reintegration of the Many into the One" (Ruthven 75). This reductionist
approach can be found in Joseph Campbell's influential work *The Hero With
a Thousand Faces*, which actually intensifies this reductive approach by
trying to locate "the Archetype behind the archetypes, what Campbell calls
the 'monomyth' " (Ruthven 75). Campbell reduces the thousand heroes to
one, and the adventure of the hero becomes "a magnification of the formula
represented in the rites of passage: *separation-initiation-return*; which might
be named the nuclear unit of the monomyth" (Campbell 30). Another ex-
tensively used monomyth is the quest myth, which Northrop Frye identified
"as the central myth of literature and the source of all literary genres"
(Ruthven 76).

Archetypal criticism can, therefore, create a narrow perspective that literally eliminates the text: "The archetype, then, leads a life rather like the
boulder of Sisyphus, deliberately strained time after time to the top of the
cliff, only to quiver for a moment, disappear out of control, and demand
that the process be begun all over again" (Gould 23). The application of
archetypal approaches must remain as much as possible within the framework
of textual possibilities in order to avoid erroneous interpretations that are
not based on the text. Teachers and students need to bear in mind the "fact
that archetype/myth must be interpretable for it to exist and to exert any
power at all" (Gould 33). Archetypal approaches to literature prove most
valuable when they contribute to an interpretation supported by the text
itself.

Classroom Context and Teacher Preparation

The method presented in this essay is specifically designed for use in literature-in-translation courses that encompass a wide variety of topics. These
courses can also be comparative in nature, since they often include works
from different national literatures. *One Hundred Years of Solitude* is a multifaceted work, and it can be read in a wide variety of courses. One example
is a course designated Myth and the Novel. Literature-in-translation courses
often draw students from different disciplines; such students' knowledge of
literature varies, and their interpretive skills are relatively unsophisticated.

Although the levels of students enrolled in these courses vary, the primary audience for this critical approach consists of second-year (sophomore) students who have had some exposure to literature and literary analysis, acquired in English composition or introduction to world literature courses.

Textually based archetypal approaches to literature can prove especially beneficial at this level, because they afford students the opportunity to examine a text from an internal-external perspective that maintains the integrity of the text. Students at this level need ideas and concepts that they can first identify and then apply to the texts in relation to their own experience. Archetypal approaches also help bridge the gap between the students and the teacher, since their respective backgrounds and experiences are different.

To gain access to the students' beliefs, ideas, and values and then to relate some of these areas to the critical approach and the text, teachers can devise a survey form that contains a variety of general cultural and specific literary questions. The following sample questions can yield valuable information before the text is read:

1. What is your general concept of Latin America?
2. What does the term *Third World country* mean to you?
3. What is the difference between a best-seller and a literary classic?
4. Do you like to read? If so, what kinds of things do you prefer to read?
5. Who is your favorite writer? Who is your favorite singer?
6. Do you admire any person as a role model? Why?
7. What does the term *archetype* mean to you?
8. Do you know who Carl Jung is?
9. What does the term *myth* mean to you?
10. What does the title *One Hundred Years of Solitude* suggest to you?

This survey also activates the students' discourse about the text before studying it. Specific questions related to the critical method help the teacher frame the presentation of the critical approach.

Archetypal approaches do not require the teacher to be a specialist in this area. The teacher should, however, possess some knowledge of the textual levels set out above. The students should realize that archetypal approaches focus on the text from an outside perspective and belong to the subtextual level. If the method is situated in relation to the text, the students are better equipped to apply this method in a structured manner.

The teacher must have various definitions of myth and some basic notions concerning myth criticism in order to establish the place of archetypal criticism within the general field of myth criticism. The teacher should also distinguish between Freudian and Jungian psychology. Specifically, the teacher should differentiate between the function of myth and the function of archetypes in Freud and Jung to avoid possible confusion between them.

Another area in which the teacher must be knowledgeable involves the early works of García Márquez, which contributed to the writing of *One Hundred Years*. The two principal works are *Leaf Storm* and the short story "Big Mama's Funeral." These two works not only constitute important steps leading to *One Hundred Years* but provide archetypal models that appear in the novel.

Another facet of the teacher's preparation is the contextualization of the novel in various ways before the students commence their reading. This process includes a knowledge of psychology, García Márquez's literary biography, literary theory beyond the specific approach, and relevant events in Colombian and Latin American history. The last area is useful when archetypal events—such as founding a city, establishing a family dynasty, and waging endless civil wars—are examined. Finally, the teacher should be acquainted with the Bible, which plays an important role in the novel. The teacher preparation outlined here can be accomplished by consulting readily available sources.

Starting Points

As Peter J. Rabinowitz writes, the reading of a literary text can start at different points:

> One can study interpretation in terms of what happens *after* reading has finished, taking more or less completed interpretations as a starting point. One can also look at what happens *while* the process of reading is taking place. I concentrate on an earlier phase, moving one step further back to see what happens *before* the act of reading even starts.   (1–2)

The teacher must devise techniques to move students from diachronic reading, which focuses on the story, to synchronic or vertical reading, which concentrates on analysis and interpretation. Teachers can use various strategies before reading *One Hundred Years* to enhance students' dialogic interaction with the text. The underlying principle is what the Russian critic Mikhail Bakhtin terms heterophony, the diversity of voices:

> According to Bakhtin, there are many voices to be heard in a piece of creative literature. The reader chooses among these voices within the specific set of circumstances of each act of reading. Bakhtin argues convincingly that dialog lies at the heart of all human creativity with language.   (Di Pietro 112)

First, the teacher can have the students write their own definitions of myth. These can be drawn from the survey or the students can write new definitions. The aim is to correct the popular idea of myth as a false story and to afford the students the opportunity to compare their own definitions in class. The teacher should collect all the definitions, compile a list, and then distribute it to the students. The teacher can then use the students' list in conjunction with another one drawn from other sources as the basis for discussing myth and situating the idea of archetypes within the scope of myth criticism. This initial step can help frame archetypal approaches for students; above all, it constitutes the first interactive stage in studying the novel.

The second step before reading the text involves a technique called discourse before text, in which the students perform several operations, including working through "a scenario based on the theme of the reading selection" (Di Pietro 115). The teacher can select passages from *One Hundred Years* that relate to different archetypal figures or patterns and then ask the students to place themselves in the same situation and write a scenario. One example is the quest myth based on José Arcadio Buendía's journey that culminates in the founding of Macondo. The same procedure can be applied to the characters of José Arcadio Buendía and Ursula Iguarán. The teacher can ask the students to write a scenario centering on their roles as the founders of a new town based on the following passage:

> Within a few years Macondo was a village that was more orderly and hard-working than any known until then by its three hundred inhabitants. It was a truly happy village where no one was over thirty years of age and where no one had died.   (18)

In each case,

> the text you are reading is transformed into a discourse in which you have become an active participant. It is immaterial that you may never find yourself in a similar situation in real life. What is important is that the literary artist has involved you in this one.   (Di Pietro 113)

Definition framing and prereading scenarios provide initial dialogic interaction between readers and the text and convert the passive activity of reading into active involvement. These two steps also help establish the framework in which archetypes are examined in relation to the text; that is, the students can see the archetypes functioning in the text in a concrete manner.

Definitions

The definition of *archetype* must furnish students with a clear, concise concept that they can apply to *One Hundred Years*. First, the teacher should point out that Jung's theory of archetypes is a "controversial way of looking at the old and still unsolved problem of how it comes about that societies remote from one another in time and place may nevertheless invent pretty much the same stories" (Ruthven 23). At this point, the teacher can introduce examples of myths—such as the creation, the deluge, and quest myths—from different cultures or ask the students to supply them. These examples provide the basis for introducing Jung's concept of the collective unconscious.

The teacher should explain that it was primarily "the striking similarities between the myths, symbols, and mythological figures of widely separated peoples and civilizations that led Jung to postulate the existence of a collective unconscious" (Wiener 312). Jung noted that the content of this collective unconscious manifested itself through what he termed *archetypes*. Not only do these archetypes appear in myths and fairy tales, but they are also present in dreams and the products of fantasy.

Here the teacher should differentiate between Freud and Jung and the significance of the unconscious for each. Both Freud and Jung considered myth, dreams, and fantasies as products of the unconscious, but Jung did not believe that the unconscious was a reservoir of repressed personal experiences. For Jung these archetypal figures and images were never conscious and, therefore, could never have been repressed. Since archetypes refer to something fundamentally unconscious, their ultimate meaning is impossible to discern. For Jung, then, "myths are the expressions of a primordial psychic process that may even precede the advent of the human race" (Wiener 313). Although archetypes cannot be easily interpreted, Jung did work with some categories of archetypes.

Jung posits two large classes of archetypes, one related to situations and the other to figures. Jung did not often deal with archetypal situations but concentrated on figures. He enumerates six principal figures: the shadow, the anima-animus, the mother, the child, the maiden, and the wise old man. These figures are bipolar:

> they have a positive and a negative aspect, and so are capable of either helping or hurting. They appear over and over again in myths as well as in dreams, fantasies and visions. They have a way of interpenetrating each other, and so are difficult to isolate. They cannot be reduced to a simple formula.   (Hudson 185)

This definition of *archetypes* emphasizes the difficulty of interpretation posed by this approach, and the validity of Jung's theory "depends on his hypothesis of the collective unconscious and its autonomous, numinous archetypes" (Hudson 195). This definition also points out the analytical possibilities of archetypes in the study of a literary work. Students must remember that archetypes can be arbitrarily applied and may lead to false interpretations.

Students must remain within the boundaries of the text if archetypal approaches are to make a substantial contribution to their study of the text.

Archetypal Figures

One Hundred Years presents four characters whom students can analyze in relation to archetypal figures: José Arcadio Buendía, Ursula Iguarán, Colonel Aureliano Buendía, and Melquíades. The students themselves can derive the archetypal qualities of the characters by constructing an archetypal portrait of each one. The teacher can assign specific characters to pairs of students, who create the archetypal portrait based on references in the novel. Each pair keeps a detailed list of the references and page numbers. Assigning an archetypal label beforehand to each character is essential in guiding the students in their efforts without forcing them to find what is not present in the text. Ursula can be labeled the great mother, José Arcadio Buendía can be considered the patriarch, Melquíades can be linked to the image of the wise old man, and Colonel Aureliano Buendía can be seen as the warrior-hero.

The teacher should make the students aware that these characters possess traits that may contradict archetypal images. For example, José Arcadio Buendía is "a kind of youthful patriarch who would give instructions for planting and advice for the raising of children and animals, and who collaborated with everyone, even in the physical work, for the welfare of the community" (17). But he is also a man "whose unbridled imagination always went beyond the genius of nature and even beyond miracles and magic" (11). In this way, the students realize that they cannot achieve a perfect correspondence between the character and the archetypal figure.

Archetypal Patterns

In this category we can include the archetypal motifs of creation, circular time, paradise, the quest myth, the family, and the biblical pattern from Genesis to Apocalypse and the idea of Macondo as the seat of time and myth. In considering *One Hundred Years*, we also need to include the archetypal pattern of discovery, conquest, and settlement of the New World. These patterns are general in nature and emerge as readers start to synthesize and combine the macroelements of the novel. The teacher must contextualize these motifs for the students so that their reading is focused. The students already have some experience with archetypal patterns, based on the scenarios they wrote involving the quest myth and José Arcadio Buendía's journeys. It is absurd to expect students to detect all these patterns; in view of the wide variation in readers' experiences, trying to teach them all could result in a mechanical application of archetypal patterns to the novel. Therefore, the teacher should, as in the case of archetypal figures, draw up a list of possible patterns on which small groups of students (two to four) can focus.

In a novel the reader establishes a hierarchy of detail; that is, not all its features have equal weight. Therefore, teachers need to be specific in making reading assignments about a specific pattern. Group work on the text helps maintain a concentrated and balanced focus on the text, so that the students' conclusions are drawn primarily from the textual reading.

If the assignment is to see how the paradise motif functions in the novel, the teacher can use the following procedure to move the students from object-regulation (simply mastering the mechanics of reading the text) to self-regulation, in which the reader "is able to evaluate the work in terms of his or her own opinion and then come to a personal conclusion about the work's extended meaning and its effect on the reader" (Di Pietro 111). The teacher should avoid other-regulation in which "students are in sufficient control of the mechanics of the text to be able to respond to the teacher's commentaries and judgments of it as literature" (Di Pietro 111). The teacher can give students the discourse-before-text assignment based on several descriptions of Macondo in the first chapters. The entire group should write the scenario; the teacher can then read it and make further suggestions. The next step is to assign the first two chapters of *One Hundred Years*, in which the main elements of Macondo's paradisiacal stage appear. The teacher can also assign Genesis in the Bible or other appropriate passages to enhance the discussion of the idea of paradise. The third step, culminating in self-regulation, consists of having the group present its project to the other students, who then discuss the concept of paradise as it appears in the novel. Discussion can then shift to a comparison between the novel and the biblical versions of paradise. This procedure leads to the students' dialogic interaction with the text, maintains the central textual focus, and concentrates the readers' attention on prominent textual features. Above all, it gives concrete expression to archetypal patterns and shows how they function in the novel.

Synthesizing Archetypes, Literary Texts, and Literary Analysis

Archetypal approaches to *One Hundred Years* afford students the opportunity to deepen their understanding of the novel beyond the textual boundaries, but this critical focus can be applied to the detriment of both the students and the text. The teacher must use archetypal approaches "only as far as the structure and potential meaning of the work consistently support such approaches" (Guerin 192). The teacher shows the students how their individual analyses of archetypal figures and patterns interrelate and how archetypal criticism fits into the broader analytical framework for studying the novel.

The teacher can start by reminding the students that the first page of *One*

Hundred Years introduces the primary archetypal figures. This point is important, since the beginnings, the endings, and the titles of novels often occupy privileged positions in relation to the rest of the work. A short review of their characteristics demonstrates which traits may legitimately be termed *archetypal.* The next step involves situating the characters in relation to the family. The teacher can not only stress the roles of Ursula Iguarán and José Arcadio Buendía as those of the great mother and the patriarch but also underscore their roles as the archetypal couple whose descendants are repetitions of them. The teachers should point out the mind-body duality in José Arcadio Buendía that the male descendants continue. The female descendants, however, present more variety, since outside women also contribute to the Buendía clan. Having linked archetypal figures to a unit, the teacher can then focus on their activities, such as founding a city, establishing a family, undertaking journeys, and engaging in endless civil wars. These activities must be contextualized within an archetypal framework characterized by repetition and circularity:

> There was no mystery in the heart of a Buendía that was impenetrable for her [Pilar Ternera] because a century of cards and experience had taught her that the history of the family was a machine with unavoidable repetitions, a turning wheel that would have gone on spilling into eternity were it not for the progressive and irremediable wearing of the axle.   (364)

By synthesizing all these areas—archetypal figures, patterns, and context —the teacher furnishes students with a model for their own efforts in arriving at their own syntheses and reaching the goal of self-regulation.

To situate archetypal-myth criticism within a broader scope, the teacher can point out that this approach

> offers some unusual opportunities for the enhancement of our literary appreciation and understanding. An application of myth criticism takes us far beyond the historical and aesthetic realms of literary study—back to the beginning of mankind's oldest rituals and beliefs. (Guerin 191)

Archetypal criticism offers the students a way of understanding human experience and its literary expression. The teacher must take care, however, that students' "enthusiasm for a new-found interpretive key does not tempt [them] to discard other valuable critical instruments or to try to open all the literary doors with this single key" (Guerin 191). Several examples from *One Hundred Years* can help clarify this point.

The picture of Macondo's paradisiacal stage can also be interpreted in political terms as a socialist vision of equality:

> José Arcadio Buendía . . . had set up the placement of the houses in
> such a way that from all of them one could reach the river and draw
> water with the same effort, and he had lined up the streets with such
> good sense that no house got more sun than another during the hot
> time of day.   (18)

In the same vein, the biblical deluge in the novel, which symbolizes renewal
and a new beginning, can be understood differently in political terms. The
Buendía family, which has another chance to change the bankrupt policies
of the Liberals (represented by Colonel Aureliano Buendía) and the Conservatives (whose values are embodied by Fernanda del Carpio), continues
along the same path. This is why "races condemned to one hundred years
of solitude did not have a second opportunity on earth" (383). These examples
help students understand that archetypal criticism can best enhance their
understanding of *One Hundred Years* in combination with other perspectives. In other words, the most fruitful application of the archetypalist perspective is a textually based one that enables students to interact dialogically
with the text. Archetypes thus lose their essentialist aura and become one
of the polyphonic voices that come from the text. The techniques described
here are designed to encourage this dialogic interaction so that students can
arrive at self-regulation and so that the potentially vague idea of archetypes
is converted into a concrete expression of the text's meaning.

An Approach from Analytical Psychology

Gary Eddy

> . . . they learned that dominant obsessions can prevail
> against death. . . .
>
> *One Hundred Years of Solitude*

I teach *One Hundred Years of Solitude* in modern-novel courses and creative-writing courses at second- and third-year levels and at the graduate level. My approach can be used at earlier levels of instruction and in humanities or similar interdisciplinary courses. This essay first explores and defines an approach using analytical psychology and then applies the theory to the novel. An appendix briefly discusses ways the characters may be interpreted and how learners may be led to their own discoveries and connections.

An approach using principles of analytical psychology offers learners a framework that can produce a totalizing and coherent reading of *One Hundred Years of Solitude*. It can also work in concert with other texts in an epic tradition and with texts that emphasize the psychological or mythic facets of heroic journeys. I emphasize *epic* here because *One Hundred Years* can be seen as a journey through time, rather than space, a fourth-dimensional quest tale. It is an example of a negative quest; the hero does not steal the fire of the gods but, rather, seeks the fulfillment of his fate, even if that fate is dissolution of consciousness. This approach can lead learners to explanations for the downward spiral of the novel as it moves inexorably toward the extinction of the Buendía family.

Like all quests, *One Hundred Years* is analogous to the struggle of the soul for individuation and higher integration. Whereas in the epic tradition the energy of the community (including the reader) is focused on a specific hero, Gabriel García Márquez presents a family through six generations with a significant warning about the state of the modern psyche. The Buendía family is the hero of this journey. But the story of the family, with its recurring obsessions and taboos, is a model of a single consciousness on a tragic quest, doomed because it is forever unable to integrate the everpresent contents and images of the unconscious into its waking life. As such, the novel can be approached from the point of view of analytical psychology.

The three concepts from analytical psychology (primarily the work of Carl G. Jung and Erich Neumann) that shed the most light on the psychological processes the novel portrays are the uroboros (or great round, the snake swallowing its tail), the *temenos* (an enclosed space such as a courtyard or a house), and the archetype of the mother.

According to Neumann, the uroboros is the symbol of the ego immersed in the unconscious. It is the image of origin, the primal condition of the psyche before it discovers its subjectivity and individuality, and it is a central symbol of the alchemical tradition, a symbol invited into the novel by the wealth of alchemical references. "The uroboros of the maternal world is life and psyche in one; it gives nourishment and pleasure, protects and warms, comforts and forgives. It is the refuge for all suffering, the goal of all desire" (*Origins* 1: 15). I view *One Hundred Years* as the saga of a single psyche enclosed in a primal circle where the images of the unconscious appear, where the miraculous is taken for granted, where "[t]he world was so recent that many things lacked names" (11), and where the struggle of the self to become fully conscious begins.

The uroboros, as the origin of consciousness, is both creative and devouring. It is the source of the archetypes that shape consciousness, that provide the "dominant obsessions [that] can prevail against death" (378): alchemy, building in order to destroy, incest, war, sexuality. And it devours the spirits of those who fail to break away from the house or who return, as if to sleep, to indulge pointless pleasures, or to repeat themselves to death.

Neumann tells us, too, that the uroboros is a combination of fecundating (male) and nurturing (female) elements (*Mother* 20). Both positive and negative male and female energies coexist in this undifferentiated psyche. The person in an uroboric state is seen as totally unconscious, as an infant who has not yet seen beyond the breast of the mother. The fertility of this undifferentiated male-female psychic realm is expressed in the number of children throughout the book, the proliferation of affairs and marriages, even the fecundity of Aureliano Segundo's and Petra Cotes's animals. The uroboros, the snake that swallows itself tail first, creates to express itself, but it also creates to fill itself. However, what it creates is apprehended by consciousness as images of archetypes from the collective unconscious, activated by the psyche's need for balance; these images are projected onto others or onto one's surroundings and, thus, made psychically real.

The structure of the novel itself is uroboric. The identity of the narrator is not revealed until the final pages. Melquíades is the speaker, and the book is his prophecy. The book we read is the book at the center of the house; as we complete the novel, we discover its origins. The novel is circular; the snake swallows its tail.

At the center of the novel's projected psyche is the stage on which all the events are played out: the house. In this enclosed space the characters meet their obsessions and face the archetypes that run through their family like water through a dry riverbed. Jung would call the Buendía house a *temenos*, "a taboo area where [one] will be able to meet the unconscious." Jung writes further:

> The drawing of a spellbinding circle is an ancient magical device used by anyone who has a . . . secret purpose in mind. . . . The same procedure has also been used since olden times to set a place apart as holy and inviolable: in founding a city, for instance, they first drew the

sulcus primigenius or original furrow.   ("Individual Dream Symbol-ism" 334)

In the great round of the novel's incipient psyche, the Buendías draw their original furrow, their house, wherein all the inhabitants encounter the family's, their own, and their community's unconscious. The meeting with the unconscious is how the uroboric contents are integrated into the psyche and become tools for growth, rather than mysterious tyrants of behavior. Here the archetypes of the numerous José Arcadios, Remedioses, Amarantas, and Aurelianos surface and submerge. The house contains the souls of all Buendía family members, living and dead, and the decaying ghosts of Melquíades and Prudencio Aguilar. If the souls of the Buendía family are to meet and devour the dragons of the uroboros, they can do it only in the house, their sacred space.

As both Jung and Neumann assert in several places and as Gaston Bache-lard notes, the enclosure of the *temenos* is associated with shelter, protection, and is seen as an expression of the primary characteristics of the archetypal feminine or great mother (Neumann, *Mother* 45–46). Ursula, the matriarch and the focus of the life in the house, oversees the energy transformations inside the *temenos*. In Bachelard's terms she protects the reverie and the creative potential of the people inside the house. To view Ursula in terms of the energies she contributes to the family and the attributes she bears from the archetypal feminine is to understand the novel's prime mover. The images and the attitudes she embodies rule the novel and dominate the characters' psychic lives.

In the central consciousness of *One Hundred Years*, the strongest pro-jections are of women: mother-matriarch (Ursula, Santa Sofía de la Piedad), virgin (Amaranta, Remedios the Beauty), and whore-witch (Pilar Ternera and, by inference, Petra Cotes). These three types and their variations isolate three main characteristics: the power to fight off the chaos of the outside world, the restraint that enforces the incest taboo or that symbolizes oth-erworldly and spiritual virtues, and the tides of fertility and sexuality that move the family forward. The house is run by Ursula or Santa Sofía de la Piedad, or it is not run at all—strong support for the relation between the mother archetype and the *temenos*. Whenever the house is literally falling apart (except for the deluge that destroyed the entire town), either Fernanda or Amaranta Ursula is in charge.

The powerful woman figure is always the source of growth, wealth, success, and fertility for the Buendía family. Neumann—in his study of the archetype, *The Great Mother*—calls this psychological and biological force "the ele-mentary characteristic of the Archetypal Feminine":

Everything born of it belongs to it and remains subject to it; and even if the individual becomes independent, the Archetypal Feminine relativizes this independence into a non-essential variant of her own essential being.   (25)

This force is profoundly conservative, as are Ursula and Santa Sofía de la Piedad.

The matriarchal force in the novel acts like a gravitational field. Though it keeps the household together, it also draws the children deeper and deeper into unconsciousness, into the undifferentiated uroboros. It is a vehicle of the doom predicted by Mequíades's scrolls. García Márquez describes the force with a cosmic image of Aureliano Segundo: "a wandering star in Ursula's planetary system" (245). Colonel Aureliano Buendía, an ego struggling against this gravity to assert itself, ends by surrendering, exhausted from fighting the Conservatives. He returns to a state of complete withdrawal and obsession: making gold fishes, only to melt them down and begin again. This recessive trait surfaces again in the household, as do obsession with the manuscripts, incestuous attraction, dalliances with Pilar Ternera. Each repetition represents the rise to consciousness of uroboric psychic contents. Building in order to destroy is a fitting symbol of the negative, devouring aspect of the mother archetype (just as the Hindu mother goddess Maya creates the children of the world, only to devour them later). Its recurrence shows that the unconscious content has not been integrated, that the child cannot grow up.

Neither the archetypal feminine nor Ursula exerts solely negative force on the characters; both also have a "transformative character" (Neumann, *Mother* 24–38).

Ursula, as the center of the family, is a transformative figure. She is teacher, cook, seamstress, and counselor. Neumann calls these occupations the foundation of culture and transformative traits; they change the material world, paralleling their power to change the world of the psyche (*Mother* 59). Ursula is the first to break out of the primal circle of Macondo, connecting it to the outside world, and to discover the sea. Petra Cotes shows that not only the matriarchs can be transformative. She is the inventor of the raffles, a model of the medieval Fortuna figure, who changes Aureliano Segundo from a brooding Aureliano type into an outgoing José Arcadio type:

> Nature had made him reserved and withdrawn, with tendencies toward solitary meditation, and she had molded an opposite character in him, one that was vital, expansive, open, and she had injected him with a joy for living and a pleasure in spending and celebrating until she had converted him, inside and out, into the man she had dreamed of for herself ever since adolescence.   (193)

The power to so change another may arise from a force greater than both the transformed and the transformer: the energy of change and rebirth emanating from the uroboros.

Neumann tells us that whenever we encounter symbols of rebirth, "we have to do with a matriarchal transformation mystery" (*Mother* 59). These mysteries, like those of Eleusis, demonstrate the feminine creative principle that "woman as vessel is not made by man or out of man or used for his procreative purposes; rather, the reverse is true: it is this vessel with its mysterious creative character that brings forth the male in itself and from out of itself" (*Mother* 62). Everywhere in the novel we see rebirth: the repetition of names, tendencies, and events. These rebirth symbols balance the conservative elementary character.

These rebirths connect us again with the uroboros: "time was not passing," Ursula realizes, "it was turning in a circle" (310). Transformation "merely creates change within the circular snake of the uroboros, for the uroboros of the beginning is not only the [Great] Round but also the wheel turning upon itself and the serpent which at once bears, begets, and devours" (Neumann, *Mother* 30).

It is no wonder that in a community dominated by such transformative women we find a magical reality.

The value of this approach in the classroom is manifold. Learners bring in their own conceptions of the unconscious, the feminine, and the fully realized soul, and they make preliminary assertions about the novel as a whole and connections between the images, the archetypes, and episodes or details from the book. Learners discover how those who are born in or wander into Macondo are motivated by its unconscious forces. They look at Melquíades's alchemical parchments and mysterious experiments as models for the secrets of transformation. To this end, the instructor can remind learners that the original quest of alchemy, to change base metals into gold, is a metaphor for the transformation of the soul. The philosopher's stone that José Arcadio Buendía seeks is within him. Ideally, learners arrive at the conclusion that time may be better spent avoiding the fate the parchments proclaim than translating them. They may question why this fate is discovered only when it is fulfilled—a psychic truth for them. Or the instructor may provoke discussion of the mothers in the text, analyzing actions and attributes to arrive at a comprehensive view of the mother archetype as the novel presents it. For learners in first- or second-year courses, the connections they make in supporting those insights can be more valuable than the "correct" interpretations. All interpretations are under revision; only the means of supporting and developing them remain constant.

To see this approach in action, let's begin with incest as an uroboric phenomenon. García Márquez points out that Ursula and her husband "were joined till death by a bond that was more solid than love: a common prick of conscience. They were cousins" (28). There was "a horrible precedent" in their recent genealogy: a cousin of theirs "had been born and had grown up with a cartilaginous tail in the shape of a corkscrew and with a small tuft of hair on the tip" (28). This is the origin of the curse that Ursula spends her life trying to prevent. In the psyche that the novel presents to us, incest is the final dissolution of individuality as this psyche returns to the undifferentiated world of the unconscious. Dissolution of the ego appears in the incestuous relationship between Aureliano and Amaranta Ursula that brings Melquíades's prophecy to fulfillment.

Amaranta Ursula and Aureliano are described as totally abandoned to their sexuality: "They lost their sense of reality, the notion of time, the rhythm of daily habits" (372). They destroy the house and refuse to go outside it. Neumann equates incest with "death ecstasy" and remarks:

> Sexuality here means losing the ego and being overpowered by the female, which is a typical, or rather archetypical experience in puberty. Because sex is experienced as the all-powerful transpersonal phallus and womb, the ego perishes and succumbs to the supreme fascination of the nonego. The Mother is still too great, the seat of unconscious too near for the ego to resist the surge of the blood. (*Origins* 61)

And García Márquez points out clearly that Aureliano has succumbed:

> [I]t was Amaranta Ursula who ruled in that paradise of disaster with her mad genius and her lyrical voracity, as if she had concentrated in her love the unconquerable energy that her great-great-grandmother had given to the making of little candy animals. (373)

Thus, the consciousness formerly given over to the manuscripts and to deciphering fate dissolves in sexuality. It is perhaps the closest thing to profound love we see in the novel, and it marks the downfall of the family. What do learners make of the message hidden in this irony?

Viewing the novel as an attempt by a psyche to escape the maternal uroboros and to individuate can provide learners with insight into the regressions that many characters live out when they return to the house. It can also explain the tragic encounters with the outside world.

The uroboros is a container of the collective traits of the family, but it is also a barrier. Any influence from the outside that violates the circle drawn around the family can either face destruction by the collective (best seen in Fernanda's progressive dissolution of consciousness) or wreak devastating changes on the collective. The most powerful outside force to violate the circle is the banana company. "Endowed with means that had been reserved for Divine Providence in former times, they changed the pattern of the rains, accelerated the cycle of harvest, and moved the river . . ." (214).

The town is transformed from without, and only a four-year deluge can clean up the excesses of the banana company.

The barrier effect of the circle profoundly affects its inhabitants as well. The gypsies, archetypal outsiders, seduce José Arcadio Buendía with their fervor for the arcane. Until this time, he is depicted as the patriarch and the chief consultant on matters of law, religion, and domestic efficiency. But once he succumbs to the alchemists and their novelties, he abandons responsibility to the collective and turns away from his family. He is pulled down into a dreamlike state made up of the unconscious contents of the uroboros. This tendency, like exogamy, may not be negative. He may be moving toward the assertion and the assimilation of these buried contents —discovering the philosopher's stone and, thus, becoming the person who renews the collective. But José Arcadio Buendía experiences, on the contrary, a complete dissolution of personality—madness. An external force contaminates the uroboric contents and endangers the individual. Jung describes the problem of diminishing morality in an expanding society in his essay "The Relations between the Ego and the Unconscious":

> The morality of society as a whole is in inverse ratio to its size; for the greater the aggregation of individuals, the more the individual factors are blotted out, and with them morality, which rests entirely on the moral sense of the individual and the freedom necessary for this.   (100)

The larger Macondo becomes, the more external forces enter the uroboros, and the less responsible, constructive, and creative the society becomes. Any element that violates the circle disrupts the inner harmony of the encircled contents.

Leaving the circle can be equally devastating to the individual and to the collective. The danger lies in bringing back new psychic contents to the circle before the original ones are assimilated and brought to consciousness. What usually follows when the men leave is adventure, education, even greatness. But when they return, they are consumed by the uroboros. José Arcadio leaves and travels six times around the world, living out his father's ambition—a positive step. He returns as a tattooed barbarian to wallow in indolence and sensuality, abandoning any future growth. His death is inevitable. We see the same fate in the colonel. As soon as he returns to the circle, he withdraws as if into a womb and makes his delicate golden fishes. In contrast, the women who leave and return bring change in their wake. Ursula—after her search for José Arcadio that results in her discovery of the sea, her husband's original quest—is followed by "peddlers of everyday reality. They came from the other side of the swamp, only two days away, where there were towns . . ." (43). She opens the way for the banana company, the railroad, and all the other contaminants of the uroboros. In either case, it is not the breaking of the circle that is dangerous—in fact, it may represent real psychic progress—but the return to the circle.

By its nature Macondo is a metaphor for Eden, and *One Hundred Years* is a history of the world. The uroboros is a unity, and an uroboric novel gives us a Genesis-to-Revelation study of the tensions between the forces of birth and death, of gravity and freedom in the great round. Learners sense this unity in themselves. We can place ourselves inside the microcosm and succumb to its taboos and miracles because the uroboros contains us. Macondo's reality is ours.

We are drawn to this history of the world for two reasons. First, it is fundamentally unified and is, therefore, more accessible than the terrifyingly ambiguous world in which we live. Second and more important, it presents us with a world more real than our daily one because *One Hundred Years* is a construction of both conscious and unconscious elements. The personalities and the events that surface here have greater definition because they irrupt from the undifferentiated unconscious of the uroboros, the container of opposites, to take conscious shape. The magical realism of the novel presents both sides of the psyche, whereas realism presents only the conscious contents in order to discover the unconscious beneath them. Both methods are valuable, but, for readers who are aware of the influence of the unconscious in their own lives, García Márquez's strategy may be the more holistic and natural one.

The uroboric novel is a parallel of the mind and can be interpreted in many of the same ways a mind is interpreted. We can identify with the novel as a whole psyche more readily than we can with any one character. Indeed, we never have any one central character with whom to identify. A character here is not our metaphor for self but, rather, a vehicle for recognizing traits in ourselves. The novel teaches us many things about the nature of the conscious mind and its relations with its shadowy sister, the unconscious. We learn from the novel that we create our own ethics and must face the consequences of not living by them. The novel also embodies the psychic fact that each of us must explore the self, translate it from its impenetrable coded Sanskrit, and assimilate the contents of the unconscious we discover before we can step out of the circle into the world.

APPENDIX

The following are interpretive statements on the central characters, the archetypes, in *One Hundred Years of Solitude*. Instructors may use them for discussion or integration into writing projects.

Ursula: She provides the central thread of the novel and represents the force of the great mother in both the elementary and the transformative characters. The notable attributes of the positive or good mother are "maternal solicitude and sympathy; the magic authority of the female; . . . all that is benign, all that fosters growth and fertility. The place of magic transformation (*temenos*) and rebirth, together with the underworld and its inhabitants, are presided over by the mother" (Jung, "Psychological Aspects" 16). Yet her protective energy draws the family members back to the house-womb-unconscious, where they ultimately regress and perish.

José Arcadio Buendía: The founder of Macondo, the patriarch, he has the obsession with alchemy and the rationalization of the miraculous that lead him to psychic fragmentation and enchainment to the chestnut tree, which can be interpreted as the tree at the center of the world, the protective aspect of the vegetation mother goddess, or as the Osiris-Woden-Christ tree of suffering and sacrifice. His is the male principle that runs through the family in fragmented form: contemplative and spiritual or active and self-indulgent.

The Aureliano type: These men—"withdrawn, but with lucid minds" (174)—are the interpreters of Melquíades's scrolls. They may, once outside the *temenos*, become men of action, but within it they surrender their psychic gains. The travels away from the house get shorter and shorter until for Aureliano Segundo they amount to a trip across town to Petra Cotes's house.

The José Arcadio type: These are the self-indulgent men of action, already alienated from their animas, who must end violently—"impulsive and enterprising, but they were marked with a tragic sign" (174). Both types are inherently incomplete and doomed by this limited inheritance.

Pilar Ternera: The other matriarch, she bears all the signs of the witch persona of the mother archetype: seducer, intoxicater, clairvoyant, fate. She is the impetus for both the colonel and his brother to explore the lighted world outside Macondo. She is the adviser to the male children of the family and the negative image of Ursula. The dynamic of these two matriarchs propels the male characters.

Other female characters: They seem to be fragments of the mother archetype, as the male characters are fragments of the father. Amaranta: virgin-Sophia (the medieval goddess), ascetic denial coupled with seductiveness; Petra Cotes: Fortuna, fertility; Remedios the Beauty: virginity, inspiration, Artemis; Amaranta Ursula: sexual ecstasy, dissipation, Astarte; Santa Sofía de la Piedad: nurturing self-effacement. Reducing women characters to functions and ciphers is (1) sexist, (2) incomplete and reductive, and (3) an oversimplification of the characters García Márquez has drawn, but their functions in the matriarchal field of the house are clear and show the completeness of the archetype's representation in the novel.

Hermeneutics: A Phenomenological Approach

Mario J. Valdés

The separation of fictional accounts of the past from historical studies is a legacy from a positivistic period when the bias against literature was notorious. That this separation is grounded in a questionable distinction between the objective truth of history and the subjective experience of literature is lamentable in the late twentieth century. A number of philosophers and historians—not least of whom are Paul Ricoeur, Hayden White, and Louis O. Mink—have effectively argued the ontological limitations of empirical research in history. Today a new generation of students are embarking on the study of literature and history, and we must give them the advantage of a philosophically informed method of study, rather than prolong the failure of historicism, which has isolated and separated works of fiction from the real world, the world of action.

A phenomenological approach to the study of literature does not blur the disciplinary lines between history and literature; it brings them together as complementary partners in the study of historical reality. This approach recognizes history as the documentary examination of the past to project an imaginative reenactment of what probably happened in the past. By contrast, fiction is the imaginative configuration of data into a portrait of what may have been in the past. These two projects are not contradictory; they are complementary, for what probably happened in the past can be called only from what may have been in the past.

Criticism of *One Hundred Years of Solitude* presents an exemplary case study of the ravages that historicism has brought to the study of literature. Even a cursory review of the novel's critical commentaries evinces the persistence of the two sides of this outdated argument and the weakness of both. Is this novel the creative flight of the imagination that has produced a modern classic of fantastic literature? Or is it a deeply committed ideological and historically informed view of the present state of affairs in Latin America? Those who respond that it is both under the rubric of magical realism do not respond to the basic inconsistency that such a claim has in the minds of undergraduate students. A number of studies are unencumbered with the excess baggage of historicism. The first part of this book demonstrates this observation. The phenomenological approach to teaching *One Hundred Years of Solitude* begins by attacking the disease and not its symptoms, by putting to rest the purported subject-object dichotomy in favor of a richer sense of reality as a process of world making in which the imagination builds a configuration from the empirical data and a rational extension gained through the sciences.

Instructors have many ways of teaching the phenomenological approach to the novel, and I do not claim that the method I use in this essay has superiority, only that it works. The basic method is to prepare an outline of the issues to be presented and to open up these issues through questions

—questions that do not have simple and uniform answers but that open up more and more questions. The objective is not to enclose the novel in a correct interpretation. On the contrary, the aim is to keep the novelistic inquiry open and to enrich the students' reading and help them appropriate the novel into the world of action.

I use the phenomenological approach of contemporary hermeneutics at both the undergraduate level and the graduate level in comparative literature and in Hispanic studies. Teachers can also use this approach in conjunction with other approaches, notably as a complement to a narratological examination of literary texts. Some of my colleagues use a phenomenological approach as the basis for seminar discussions of literature and advanced conversation courses.

In this essay I limit my remarks to the basic principles of the phenomenological approach. The aim of this approach is twofold: to enhance a dialogic relation between the student and the text and to enable the student to share the meaning of that relation with others—in other words, to move beyond subjective response to the reasoned presentation of that response.

The instructor first questions the cultural and ideological presuppositions of Colombia and Latin America, on the one hand, and the United States and Canada, on the other hand. Then the inquiry moves to the mode of expression and the reception of these values, thoughts, beliefs, and ideas. A third level of inquiry is the consideration of the strategies of composition and of reading that are put into play in the realization of the novel as a narrative world. The end of the questioning is a probe into the ways in which such a realization is related to the world of action, of which the classroom is merely the most immediate representative.

Here I demonstrate this approach with passages from chapter 15 of the unnumbered twenty chapters of *One Hundred Years*.

I ask eight questions that move the classroom discussion from cultural and ideological presuppositions to the specifics of response. The questions do not have simple or definitive answers; they are, above all, a way of thinking and talking about the text.

1.   *What is an event?* Events themselves are silent; they are mute confluences of collective action. Events mean something only when someone tells us what happened. We must remind ourselves that events receive an intelligibility from their place in the development of a story.

The plot of any narrative has a number of events linked in the unfolding story, whether we are dealing with novels or with history. History is the retelling of a story at least partially known to its readers. It is retelling the story backward from its conclusion to its beginning. We already know how things have turned out, but we read the historian's version because we seek to know why they turned out that way.

Historical narratives vary from complete conformity to the tradition of the plot to revision of the accepted explanation of why things turned out the way they did. Between these two extremes lie many combinations concerning the selection, emphasis, accumulation, and interpretation of events that support or challenge the purported true story. Historical accounts of events do not differ in essence from events in a novel. Only the methods of reporting differ: the novelist has a complex range of modes of reporting; the historian is relatively limited to the interpretation of documents.

2. *How does history present an event?* One of the most violent events in the twentieth-century history of Colombia was the 1928 massacre of striking United Fruit Company banana plantation workers in the town of Ciénaga. The United Fruit Company, founded in 1899 by M. C. Keith with United States capital, had extensive land holdings in Costa Rica, Guatemala, and Colombia. Within five years of incorporation, the United Fruit Company had built an empire of plantations, private railroads, and shipping fleets. The company's aggressive methods in its labor relations are well documented. The exploitation of the workers and the exaggerated profits to its United States stockholders are also well documented.

In 1928 the banana workers in the district of Magdalena were on strike because their wages were paid in company-issued notes, rather than in general currency, and because their living conditions were appalling. A rapid assessment of the company's situation throughout Latin America reassured the company executives in New York that the strike was entirely a local occurrence. The executives sent instructions to the local managers to deal with the strike rapidly and decisively, since a prolonged strike could have far-reaching negative consequences on other company holdings. The local managers ordered the army officers from Bogotá to keep the peace, to have the army serve as strikebreakers, and to eliminate the militant union leaders. The plan was simple and direct: the army would get the bananas shipped, remove the union leaders, and put fear into the workers. The strike was broken within two weeks of the arrival of the troops. The soldiers ran the trains, cut the bananas, and packed the trains. But the climactic event was the army's show of force—the massacre of 28 October 1928. The local company managers called the workers to a general meeting in the plaza of Ciénaga, not far from the larger towns of Santa Marta and Aracataca, the birthplace of García Márquez. Some three thousand men, women, and children were slaughtered when the army troops fired machine guns into the crowded plaza. The union leaders who escaped the massacre were all captured and shot in the days after the event. The magnitude of the massacre was such that the ruling Conservative government felt obliged to silence all news reports, to impose press censorship, and to offset a possible public outcry by insisting that nothing had happened in Ciénaga. Government statements assured everyone that some local malcontents had caused trouble but that the workers had been promised that the temporary lack of facilities would be attended to in the near future. The company strategy of creating fear among the workers had gone too far and was an embarrassment to the Bogotá government. However, the desire for more foreign markets for bananas and coffee remained the government priority.

The basic sources for this account are Charles David Kepner, *The Banana Empire*; Charles W. Bergquist, *Coffee and Conflict in Colombia*; and, specifically dealing with this novel and the historical event, Lucila Inés Mena, "La huelga de la compañía bananera como expresión de lo real maravilloso americano en *Cien años de soledad*"; and Gene H. Bell-Villada, "Banana Strike and Military Massacre: *One Hundred Years of Solitude* and What Happened in 1928."

3. *How does the novel present the event?* The narrative voice is an impassive observer who has full knowledge and authority over the characters and the incidents in the hundred-year story of Macondo. The narrative voice supplements general descriptions by reporting on the singular responses of various members of the Buendía family. The narrative voice's description of the incidents leading up to the event are presented with the same combination of overview and singular viewpoints.

The narrator gives a systematic buildup of the impasse. The event is not only the reenactment of a historical event but also the dramatic telling of a story. "Cultivation stopped half-way, the fruit rotted on the trees and the hundred-twenty-car trains remained on the sidings" (280). However, the narrative focus never wavers from the people participating in the event: "in the poolroom at the Hotel Jacob they had to arrange twenty-four-hour shifts" (280). The story is not an abstraction of action or a summary of causes. The narrator shifts effortlessly from the general view to the singular: "That was where José Arcadio Segundo was on the day it was announced that the army had been assigned to reestablish public order" (280). The narrator incorporates the rhetoric of governmental announcements into the description of José Arcadio Segundo as a participant in the action. The character's response to the public announcement is the response of the text: it "was like an announcement of death" (280). José Arcadio Segundo leaves the poolroom and watches the troops arrive. But the description is not his; all descriptions belong to the narrative voice and are generalized to permit the images to grow and become the reader's as well:

> Although it took them over an hour to pass by, one might have thought that they were only a few squads marching in a circle, because they were all identical, sons of the same bitch, and with the same stolidity they all bore the weight of their packs and canteens, the shame of their rifles with fixed bayonets, and the chancre of blind obedience and a sense of honor. (280–81)

The situation is fixed in the story but not in history. García Márquez must add the viewpoint of the historian. The martial law established in the district gives the army the authority to serve as mediator between the workers and the plantation administrators, but this authority was not used. Instead, the army became the strikebreakers. They did the work of the plantation: they cut the fruit, loaded the railway cars, and ran the trains. The army, by replacing the workers, take themselves out of a military function and adopt a political function. The response of the workers is to sabotage the army's sabotage of the strike. The violence begins; burning the plantations and the commissaries, tearing up the railway tracks, cutting telegraph and telephone wires, the workers fight back not against a military force but against a strike-breaking force. When the violence becomes general in the district, the North American managers and their families leave. The situation has deteriorated because of the army's political action and the workers' responses. The next move is the government's. Now that a civil war is imminent, the army is ordered back into its military function. The authorities summon the workers to gather in Macondo to be addressed by the leader of the province. Purportedly the army is to keep the peace and facilitate a political solution to the conflict. García Márquez has prepared the ground for the event; it is now a historical development, as well as a narrative feature in the story of Macondo and the Buendía family.

The narrative summary has brought the presentation to the threshold of the event itself. The buildup reflects a narrative strategy in history. The personal perspective of José Arcadio Segundo is limited to the arrival of the troops. The passage after the phrase "Martial law enabled the army . . ." (281) presents a summary of action and the action itself. The temporal break between the announcement of the governor's planned intervention and the day of his arrival is the storyteller's use of anticipation for the climactic event. The event itself is closely tied to the narrative witness, José Arcadio Segundo, just as the historian uses eyewitness testimony. The passage is part of a narrative that could be by a novelist or by a historian. The difference is that the historian would set it off as a special document. García Márquez was not the first to present the event fictionally; it appears in Alvaro Cepeda Samudio's *La casa grande*, whose second edition of 1967 has a preface by García Márquez.

4. *How can we compare the historical and the fictional accounts of an event?* In this work of fiction the discourse belongs to the narrative voice, not to the character. Historians usually distinguish their broad assessments from the experiential testimony.

A classroom close reading, whatever the theoretical basis, calls the students' attention to the subtle development of textual indicators. In the phenomenological approach the essential difference is that the students must discern between (1) their completion of indeterminate indicators and (2) the perspective of the enunciating voice and, when pertinent, the separation between seeing and saying. The narrator describes the event in *One Hundred Years* with the relentless punctuation of a clock and by the presence of José

Arcadio Segundo as a witness to the hours of waiting and the climax. The narrator does not give the character's verbal response, only his physical reaction of growing tension. The clock is the measure of this situation of waiting. At twelve o'clock, three thousand people—workers, women, and children—are gathered. The narrator describes how they are hemmed in, but the temper of the crowd is more like a fair than a political meeting. Food and drink stands have mushroomed around the square, and there is the noisy action of a market day or a celebration, in spite of the scorching tropical sun. The reader moves effortlessly into verisimilar configuration. By three o'clock a rumor runs through the crowd that the official train would not arrive until the next day. The crowd is about to disperse when an army officer on the roof of the railway station reads a decree that echoes the language of the historical incident; it does not address either the immediate situation of the crowd, which had been summoned and had been waiting all day, nor does it refer to the strike; instead, it identifies the strikers as hoodlums and authorizes the army to shoot to kill. The narrator rigorously controls the focus so that the depicted event approaches historical discourse. The political solution to the situation was to pass over the issues and to concentrate on the strikers as obstacles that were to be removed.

The narrator now begins to describe the two enormous adversaries; one makes a move, and the other makes a countermove, building up to the climax. The army has informed the strikers that they are lawless; the workers shout back their protest; the army informs them that they have five minutes to break up, or the army, which has prepared for this turn of events, will fire on them. The narration is now nearing the climax, and again it concentrates on the individual:

> José Arcadio Segundo, sweating ice, lowered the child and gave him to the woman. "Those bastards might just shoot," she murmured. . . . "You bastards!" he shouted, "take the extra minute and stick it up your ass!" (282–83)

The captain gives the order to shoot, and the soldiers at fourteen machine guns respond immediately. The description of the massacre is one of poetic horror. The narrator departs from the discourse of history and moves into the figurative discourse of fiction:

> But it all seemed like a farce. It was as if the machine guns had been loaded with caps, because their panting rattle could be heard and their incandescent spitting could be seen, but not the slightest reaction was perceived, not a cry, not even a sigh among the compact crowd that seemed petrified by an instantaneous invulnerability. (283)

García Márquez exploits the temporal lag from an individual vantage point. After the machine guns began to fire and before the effects could be heard or seen from an individual position, a few seconds passed, and these are the seconds of disbelief. The effects of the gunfire are described in terms of Latin America's most violent natural disasters—earthquakes and volcanic eruptions:

> Suddenly, on one side of the station, a cry of death tore open the enchantment: "Aaaagh, Mother." A seismic voice, a volcanic breath, the roar of a cataclysm broke out in the center of the crowd with a great potential of expansion.   (283)

But this was not a natural disaster; it was a human massacre, and the language turns from earthquake to a man-made cyclone of killing (283–84).

The author has presented the event with a hybrid discourse of history and fiction; now the consequences have to be drawn. In these circumstances the historian would draw into the account all the available supporting documentation to expand the effect. The novelist does the same by following José Arcadio Segundo's trip back to Macondo. The novel and the historical account make the same point: "The official version, repeated a thousand times" was that "there were no dead" (287). Where does this statement stand in the students' reading of the novel? Are they reading about real political action, or is this an imaginary scene?

The aftermath of the massacre is registered by the enunciating voice through the experience of a survivor, José Arcadio Segundo. Two hundred freight cars with a locomotive at either end and a third in the middle carry the three thousand dead to the sea. Once again, as at the beginning of the description of the strike, García Márquez uses the official rhetoric of government spokesmen: "There were no dead, the satisfied workers had gone back to their families, and the banana company was suspending all activity until the rains stopped" (287).

The event in both the historical account and the fictional one is given in context. The historical context is the relation of the foreign-owned company to the Colombian government, army, and local managers. The fictional context is the world of the novel, Macondo, in its development from a hamlet of three hundred persons to a large company town linked to international markets.

The event is depicted with a chronology of cause and effect in both the historical account and the fictional one. The major difference is the time frame. In the historical account the incidents of one day are dealt with in a few lines, since the economic history from 1899 to 1930 is the focus. The event in the novel takes up the major part of a chapter, although it is but one day in a hundred-year period, because the focus is on the origin, development, and destruction of a town as seen through the experiences of its founding family. Thus, the historical time frame is a macroview of action, and the novel presents a microview.

The significance of the event is drawn out in the aftermath. In the historian's version the importance of precedents and sociopolitical consequences are highlighted. In the novel the event's significance is interiorized into an aesthetic and ideological statement. The event merges into the narrative development of both the historian and the novelist but stands out as a striking example of different theses: to the historian, the United Fruit Company dominates Latin America economically and politically; to the novelist, the penalty for the failure of collective action is solitude.

5.   *How does the student respond to what is historical in the fictional account of an event?* An event in a novel is a determinate feature against which the many indeterminate features are constituted. When a historical event has been treated outside the world of the novel, the event becomes a truth-claim with great potential for ideological statements. The truth-claim in historical writing both differs from and is similar to the historical truth-claim in literature. The most obvious difference is that all references in history are to an empirical reality, a reality that is no longer but that undeniably has occurred. This absent past can be reached only through the traces available in the present, but no one who approaches the historical event doubts that a past reality existed. Thus, the paradigm of history is an intentionality to gain the past that is governed by a concept of event. But this event is not and never can be either complete or fixed; it can only be reconstituted by the historian's imagination on the basis of all the available evidence. This use of the imagination to put together the evidence is common in both history and literature. Most literary narratives are told as though they had taken place in the past; some literary texts make an explicit attempt to situate the fictional event within the known process of historical events. In these fictions the novelistic text presents the past as it was at a time previous to the act of telling the story; but, when there is a historical truth-claim, the past is not only the narrator's past internal to the novel but also the collective past of all who read, for this event is also part of the reader's historical process. The implications are profound. Not only does the novel oblige us to consider and judge values, but it also forces us to look again at our own historicity and the process we are making and remaking with each event we confront. A small village in Colombia in 1928 has suddenly become an integrated part of the student's world in the 1990s.

Thus far, I have asked the students to look at the determinate features in the novel, and I have only touched on one class of determinacies, the historical truth-claim, as it is expressed in only one passage of chapter 15. However, *One Hundred Years* includes many classes of determinate features, including empirical observations, verisimilar patterns of actions, and the intertextual use of other texts. The role of determinate features in conjunction with history is opened up for discussion.

6.   *How does the student treat indeterminate features of a text that also has determinate features from history?* Chapter 15 begins, as do the previous

fourteen chapters but not the next five, with a determinate statement concerning the history of Macondo, a history of a fictional town with specific
historical and geographical truth-claims. However, the central focus throughout the narration is not on the town itself but on the history of the Buendía
family. The first third of chapter 15 narrates Fernanda's trip with her daughter Meme to the convent in the highlands, where Fernanda had been ed-
ucated and where Meme was to end her days in self-imposed silence. This
family incident is the vehicle through which the narrator reviews the principal events of the previous fourteen chapters; this is but one of a number
of retrospective techniques that appear with increasing frequency in the
second half of the novel and that are balanced by narrative anticipations in
the first half, such as the often-quoted opening line: "Many years later . . ."
(11). Students must master the technical virtuosity of García Márquez's
narrative voice as enunciator and focalizer if they are to establish the dialogic
relation fully and not merely respond as listeners to the tale.

    In the retrospective technique of chapter 15, the entwined patterns of
verisimilar and nonverisimilar incidents pass in review. Meme is being taken
off to a convent, but along the way she continues to be engulfed in yellow
butterflies, even in the railroad carriage. The train passes through the ancient
region of enchantment, but it also passes through the banana plantations
and by the white houses of the North Americans, the North American women
dressed in shorts and striped blouses playing cards, the teams of oxen car-
rying loads of bananas along the road to the railroad terminal. We encounter
all that Meme did not see. She did not see, we are told, but this negative
focus obliges us to recognize the radical nature of the perception and the
narration in this text:

> She did not see . . . the miserable huts of the workers all huddled
> together where Mauricio Babilonia's yellow butterflies fluttered about,
> and in the doorways of which there were green and squalid children
> sitting on their pots, and pregnant women who shouted insults at the
> train.   (273)

All this has not been seen; it has been focalized and narrated as the sole
domain of the enunciating narrator. In the short space of one paragraph the
text has given us seven negative focalizations. This mixture of images both
commonplace and bizarre are what the student has encountered page after
page. How can the student reconcile the commonplace and the bizarre? The
distinctions belong to the reader; determinate features clash with indeterminate features because of their logical impertinence, but the narrative voice
presents no sign of incompatibility.

    The basic indeterminacy in the text lies with the enunciating voice and
the standpoint of focalization, which is neither inside the story—that is,
taking part or observing—nor outside the narrative, reenacting a series of

incidents from the past. A narrator inside the story would be tied to an empirical reality; a narrator outside the story would be free to engage in fantasy but only by paying the price of eliminating historical determinacies and ideological statements about them. In *One Hundred Years* the focalization always hovers over the totality of the text. The enunciating voice enacts incidents that are not merely singular but sequential, although the first-time reader may not know the sequence. The enunciating voice has narrative privilege and authority; it is a storyteller in full grasp of the whole tale at all times—much closer, in fact, to the teller of tales in an oral tradition than to the narrative voice in a written-text tradition. The narrator's authority is also disconcerting because the narration is creating archetypes, rather than psychologized fictional characters. The identity of the enunciating voice is a major cause of indeterminacy throughout the reading of all but the last chapter. Until then, the narrative source is unknown, enigmatic, and full of disconcerting mannerisms. Only in the last chapter does the narrator's identity begin to emerge as Melquíades and his internal reader emerge as Aureliano Babilonia. Instead of the usual narrative voice dramatization, this text develops the persona of a narrator embarked on a quest that takes up the entire length of the novel. Similarly, storytellers in the oral tradition reveal their identities at the end of the tale. Although the narrator's reliability is never challenged in *One Hundred Years*, the troublesome question remains: why does the narrator deliberately withhold information, such as the shooting of José Arcadio and the background of Rebeca's family when she first arrives in Macondo. The storyteller's will as manifested in what and how the narrator chooses to tell the story is the dominant feature of this text, and nothing in the natural realm of cause and effect alters this central fact and obliges or constrains the narrator. The tension between the determinate features and the numerous indeterminate aspects is in the perception of the reader, not in the narrator. Nevertheless, this tension is controlled and deftly enhanced and developed through the interweaving of the logical impertinence of the telling into a unified tale. Passage after passage, sentence after sentence shows the everpresent clash of the referential dimensions of the text. The narrative world is neither fantastic nor verisimilar; it is, rather, a metaphorical encounter of the two. This referential dialectic is not limited to certain moments in the text; it is the ontological basis of the text as experience, a metaphorical experience.

7. *What interpretation is possible when the student does not use the designations* objective *and* subjective? In a phenomenological approach the status of the text is neither objective nor subjective; it is, above all, a catalyst for the student's own thinking about reality.

Only on reflection, when we comprehend the magnitude of this tensional referentiality, do we understand the structure of the novel; it is an extended metaphor. Just as metaphor acquires its meaning through the semantic impertinence that results from the clash of the literal assigning of terms with the internal usage in a poem, so does the structure of *One Hundred Years* gain its metaphorical meaning of experience and solitude through the referential impertinence in the clash between the verisimilar and the nonverisimilar within the same enunciation uttered in the same tone by the same narrator. This clash is not occasional; it is constant. Every page augments and continues the tensional relation in the reader. This metaphorical tension is possible because of two fundamental features of the novel: the use of determinate aspects of the historical truth-claim and the indeterminate creation of focalization borrowed from the oral tradition. The result is a mesmerizing tale that insists that the price of solitude is failure in any attempt to find justice.

One Hundred Years of Solitude is a discourse with its own inner consistency as a narrative; it also has an unusual way of making references to history and to itself. The play between the determinate and indeterminate features appears to be endless. The novel is a text to be made by the reader, to be made over again with each new reading, and to be made by the student as part of a class. The classroom, as part of a larger community, is the arena for the sharing of individual experiences.

8.   *What are the basic aims of this approach in teaching literature?* A phenomenological approach to teaching literature is aimed almost exclusively at helping the student develop a personal sense of the texts so that this sense can be shared with others. The objective is not merely to help the student attain a more enriched and profound understanding of the text; that is the primary objective of all teaching. The phenomenological project in the classroom examines the individual and the community. The teacher is in the classroom to make the students fully conscious of their subjectivity in the process of living, of which literature is but a part. However, the students must transcend subjectivity if they are to communicate. Without denying or negating any aspect of the subjective experience of reading, the teacher helps each student attain an intersubjective interpretation; by using the disciplines of explanation of our understanding, the teacher encourages the student to produce an interpretation for the community, which in the first instance is the classroom. This interpretation is accessible to all, for all to agree or disagree with or to modify, but it is there among others.

A Narratological Approach

Amaryll Chanady

This essay addresses those instructors who work with graduate students, advanced fourth-year majors in comparative literature, or students in a Hispanic-studies program that stresses literary theory. Whether *One Hundred Years of Solitude* is presented in a course on the twentieth-century novel in general or in a course on the modern novel in Latin America, I have found that a narratological approach based on an exclusively immanent study of the text is less stimulating for the students than one that emphasizes the literary and sometimes nonliterary intertext from diachronic and synchronic perspectives. An intertextual approach also allows the students to appreciate the specificity of *One Hundred Years*. Therefore, I present a detailed analysis of the novel only after a brief introduction to the history of Latin American fiction; a discussion of concepts particularly relevant to the study of the novel, such as magical realism, *lo real maravilloso*, the marvelous, the fantastic, and the neofantastic; and a comparison of, for example, Miguel Angel Asturias's *Maize Men*, Alejo Carpentier's *Kingdom of This World*, and some of Julio Cortázar's short stories to illustrate these concepts. The studies of Irlemar Chiampi, Jaime Alazraki, and Floyd Merrel provide pertinent material for this part of the course. A brief comparison of the treatment of the supernatural in *One Hundred Years* and in several well-known European and American narratives (by Prosper Mérimée, Guy de Maupassant, Henry James, and Edgar Allan Poe, for example) and a succinct presentation of some major theories of the fantastic (Todorov; Bessière) allow the students to situate *One Hundred Years* in a wide literary context that may be more familiar to them than the Latin American literary tradition.

After thus situating *One Hundred Years* intertextually—with a marked emphasis on the treatment of the supernatural, which most students find particularly interesting—I explain the pertinence of the narratological approach. I treat these preliminary parts of the course in more or less depth, depending on the literary and theoretical backgrounds of the students. Class participation, stimulated by frequent questions, is usually active, since most students are acquainted with the major authors mentioned and familiar with such concepts as the fantastic and the marvelous. However, the subsequent narratological approach requires mainly a lecture format when the students are not well versed in literary theory.

While emphasizing the importance of narratology as a practical tool for analyzing a literary text, I always point out to the students that narratology addresses only one aspect of the novel. Other approaches allow us to analyze the text from different perspectives and discover facts that narratology does not take into account. Many students tend to apply narratological grids somewhat mechanically and to explain the text exclusively and even dogmatically according to a certain method. Studying various approaches in different classes often leads to compartmentalization; the students learn to apply a different method in each class without acquiring a critical distance or learning how to approach a text eclectically by selecting the most relevant analytical tools from several methods. Often, the students apply a grid that may work well for a simple narrative form but not for a complex novel. Examples of grids used in this procrustean fashion are Vladimir Propp's thirty-one functions and A. J. Greimas's *actants* and semiotic square. The grids may give an interesting perspective on the text but should be seen as abstract models that function as heuristic aids. I explain the dangers of excessive compartmentalization and reductionism to the students, for they should be aware of the limits of an approach, as well as its merits.

Notwithstanding the preceding remarks, narratology is an essential tool for explaining not only how a narrative is constructed and what formal and structural properties it shares with other narratives but also in what way it is a unique literary work of art and why it elicits certain responses from the reader. Narratology is a rigorous, well-codified methodology (or, rather, group of methodologies) that allow us to account for what we have often felt intuitively. Approaching the text neither as a historical document nor as the exclusively personal expression of the author, narratology elucidates it as an artistic verbal construct with formal properties that both situate it within a specific genre and differentiate it from other narratives.

Narratology can be divided into two main areas—the study of narrative structure, the grammar of stories (Propp; Greimas; Todorov, *Grammaire*; Bremond; Prince), and the study of the presentation or rhetoric of narration (Genette, *Figures III*; Bal, "Narration"). Jonathan Culler distinguishes between story, "a sequence of actions or events, conceived as independent of their manifestation," and discourse, "the discursive presentation or narration of events" (169–70). An exclusively structural approach is useful for analyzing the form of fairy tales—as in most of the narratological studies of Propp, Claude Bremond, Todorov, and Greimas—but it is frequently too reductionist for the analysis of longer, more complex narratives. To account for the formal properties of complex works, I find that the rhetorical approach to narratology is usually more suitable. Genette's categories of mode, voice, and time, for example, can be applied to any relatively complex narrative, except for certain experimental texts.

This twofold narratological approach can be completed by studying enunciation, the traces of the subject in discourse. Although it seems logical to include this aspect in the rhetorical approach, narratologists have generally neglected it or treated it only indirectly. The study of enunciation can constitute a method of its own (based on Benveniste and Kerbrat-Orecchioni), or it can be an integral part of discourse analysis. But since the novel contains a variety of enunciation, any rhetorical approach to narratology is incomplete without taking enunciation into account.

Because the levels and the academic backgrounds of the students vary, two problems may arise. The first problem, inevitable in any graduate course aimed at both MA and PhD students and at students from divergent academic backgrounds, is a disparity in their degree of preparation, both theoretical and literary. Although this difficulty cannot be completely eliminated, it can be appreciably attenuated in a small class group by encouraging the students to participate actively and contribute to the transmission of information. Students from different academic backgrounds can be stimulated to act as teaching aides and to share their knowledge with others. As for the difference in theoretical preparation, I usually find that advanced students lose interest less rapidly if they can explain certain concepts to less advanced students than if they listen to the instructor's explanation of what they already know. The second problem arising from teaching *One Hundred Years* to a het- erogeneous group is language. I often have groups of students reading the novel in three languages—English, French, and Spanish. Students from Hispanic studies usually prefer to read the novel in the original; francophone and anglophone students from comparative literature studies often have to rely on translations. Since there is always one basic language of instruction, all references in the class are to that particular version of *One Hundred Years*. When the translated version does not satisfactorily render the original—as often happens with connotation and level of language, which are especially significant for the analysis of enunciation—I explain the orig- inal Spanish expression.

In the main part of the course, devoted to a narratological analysis of *One Hundred Years*, I adhere largely to the narratological synthesis by Shlomith Rimmon-Kenan, accompanied by many examples from literary works. Be- sides being relatively short (132 pages, excluding notes), clearly written, and accessible to most anglophone graduate students, Rimmon-Kenan's work offers an annotated bibliography and frequent references that encourage further research. The publications on narratology are extensive, so this con- cise guide to the approach is a particularly helpful text both for those students with some knowledge of narratology and for those who have never studied the subject. This part of the course is also conducive to class participation, and I spend a considerable amount of time guiding the students in the application of concepts to *One Hundred Years* and in their analysis of relevant segments of the text.

The first distinction made by Rimmon-Kenan (a distinction based on Ge- nette) is that of story, text, and narration. The story is a chronological re- construction of the narrated events, characters, and fictional world, without consideration of the medium (style, language, manner of presentation); thus the story is an abstraction based on information given by the text. The text is the particular manner in which the events, the characters, and the fictional world are presented. Narration is the process of production (written or spoken) of the text; thus, narration concerns the narrative voice, the relation between the narrator and the story, and the representation of the characters' speech. Rimmon-Kenan points out: "Of the three aspects of narrative fiction, the text is the only one directly available to the reader. It is through the text that he or she acquires knowledge of the story (its object) and of the narration (the process of its production)" (4).

To reconstruct the story, the reader must participate actively in the concretization or actualization of the series of fictional events in chronological order and in cause-and-effect sequence. The beginning of the reconstructed story line in *One Hundred Years*, for example, coincides not with Aureliano Buendía's discovery of ice, narrated in the first paragraph of the novel, but with Sir Francis Drake's attack on Riohacha in the sixteenth century, narrated on page 27. This event caused Ursula's great-great-grandparents to leave the coastal town and move to an Indian village, where the subsequent marriage of Ursula and her cousin José Arcadio determined the subsequent course of events. The destruction of Macondo, by contrast, coincides with the end of the novel; story and text end at the same point.

I analyze the story according to various narratological models and concepts. I divide events into kernels, which advance the action, and catalysts (or satellites; see Chatman), which amplify the kernels, and combine events into microsequences, main and subsidiary story lines that involve individual characters, and macrosequences, which coincide with major sections of the plot (Barthes, "Introduction"). Although labeling events or series of events as kernels, catalysts, and microsequences always entails arbitrariness, one can frequently make a distinction between events that open an alternative (Colonel Aureliano Buendía's facing the firing squad can be considered a kernel, since the outcome determines the subsequent development of the plot in a significant way) and events that simply accompany the kernels (Aureliano's childhood memory of seeing ice for the first time is a catalyst or satellite for the above-mentioned kernel). The discovery of ice and magnets (11) can be considered a microsequence within the macrosequence of the establishment and growth of Macondo, and Aureliano's experience constitutes part of one of the main story lines involving a major character. The individual events can also be classified and named by event labels, which all readers automatically establish to concretize and understand the plot according to familiar categories (Barthes, *S/Z*). Aureliano's facing the firing squad, for example, can be labeled "threat of execution."

Claude Bremond devised a model that partially explains the dynamics of plot development. Bremond demonstrated that actions are motivated by a lack or a state of disequilibrium. The character who tries to attain a new state of equilibrium precipitates a sequence of improvement, which may coincide with a sequence of deterioration from the point of view of another character; that deterioration, in turn, precipitates a new sequence of improvement within another story line. We can, therefore, interpret the same events differently according to which perspective and story line we choose. The plot of *One Hundred Years*, for example, is set in motion by a sudden deterioration of the initial equilibrium when Drake attacks Riohacha. To improve the psychological state of Ursula's great-great-grandmother and attain a new equilibrium, the young family moves to an isolated Indian village, where their descendants cause a new state of disequilibrium by intermarrying and creating the possibility of abnormal offspring. This disequilibrium, in turn, leads to the murder of Prudencio Aguilar and precipitates the family's trek to what becomes Macondo. The murder of Prudencio can be interpreted according to the main story line of José Arcadio, who thus improves an unbearable situation, or according to the subsidiary story line of Prudencio, who wanders restlessly as a ghost and tries to improve his situation of loneliness by haunting José Arcadio.

Most structural studies of narrative demonstrate that the final equilibrium differs from the initial equilibrium. Propp's model shows a progression from, for example, the hero as a child living with his parents to the hero marrying into a new family. In his study of "Cinderella," Pierre Maranda calls the structure of initial equilibrium–negative change–final equilibrium an "inversion" or "flip-flop," and Fredric Jameson applies the expressions "exchange" and "reversal of world configurations" to the plot of the romance ("Magical Narratives"). An analysis of the macrosequences of *One Hundred Years*, however, reveals that the novel's story contains no major exchange or reversal of world configurations. The most obvious example is the destruction of the town of Macondo, which reestablishes the initial situation before the town's founding at the beginning of the story. This circular development of plot is emphasized throughout the novel. Macondo's inhabitants are just as dazzled by the "marvelous inventions" (211) introduced by Aureliano Triste and Bruno Crespi as they were when the gypsies first showed them magnets and telescopes (11–13); and Aureliano Triste's sketch of a railroad "was a direct descendent of the plans with which José Arcadio Buendía had illustrated his project for solar warfare" (209). The characters' constantly recurring names (four José Arcadios, one Arcadio, five Aurelianos within the family, and seventeen illegitimate Aurelianos engendered by the colonel during his campaigns) underscore similarities in character, a situation repeatedly emphasized by the narrator: "While the Aurelianos were withdrawn, but with lucid minds, the José Arcadios were impulsive and enterprising" (174; see also 179 and 378). Ursula realizes that "time was not passing . . . but that it was turning in a circle" (310), and Pilar Ternera believes that "the history of the family was a machine with unavoidable repetitions, a turning wheel that would have gone on spilling into eternity were it not for the progressive and irremediable wearing of the axle" (364).

For the reconstruction of character on the level of story, Greimas's concept of *actants* (sender, receiver, subject, object, helper, and opponent) is not as useful with *One Hundred Years* as with dramas and fairy tales. James Garvey's "attributive propositions," however, can easily be applied to the characters of the novel: José Arcadio Segundo, like all José Arcadios, is

impulsive and enterprising (see also Chatman's "paradigm of traits," 127).
Repetition of behavior and the "directional dimension" or character development (Rimmon-Kenan 39) complete the character construct, which is sub-
sumed under a proper name.

Story time and character are constructs based both on the text and on the
reader's experience, but text time is the "linear (spatial) disposition of linguistic segments in the continuum of the text" (Rimmon-Kenan 44). Gérard
Genette's rhetorical narratology is particularly pertinent, especially the section on order, duration, and frequency (*Figures III* 77–182). Text order is
established by the first narrative, which in *One Hundred Years* begins on
the first page of the novel with Aureliano's discovery of ice and ends on the
last page with the destruction of Macondo. The evocation of the firing-squad
episode in the first sentence of the novel is explicitly situated in the future
and can, therefore, be considered a prolepsis (Genette's term), which is
roughly equivalent to foreshadowing or anticipation. Genette, however, distinguishes between prolepsis (recounting a future event, even if only briefly)
and *amorce* (hinting at a future event). Since the first prolepsis in *One
Hundred Years* refers to an event within the time span covered by the first
narrative, it is called internal; and since it concerns the same character
(Aureliano), it is homodiegetic. An analepsis, or flashback, by contrast, provides information concerning an event that occurred in the past. The account
of Drake's attack on Riohacha, for example, is an analepsis that is both
external (referring to an event before the first narrative) and heterodiegetic
(not concerning a character described in the present and in this case not
even concerning a character within the first narrative). An example of internal
analepsis is Aureliano's prison memory of a previous assassination attempt
on him (123–24).

Genette's second temporal category, duration, refers to linear space in
the novel and can, therefore, never be equivalent to chronological duration
in story time, even in the case of direct speech. As Rimmon-Kenan points
out, it is "only by convention that one speaks of temporal equivalence of
story and text in dialogue" (52). Genette's concept of acceleration refers
to a particular temporal-spatial relation in which a short segment of text
recounts a long period of story (maximum acceleration is achieved by
ellipsis); deceleration refers to a lengthy description of a short period of
the story (Rimmon-Kenan 53). An example of appreciable acceleration in
One Hundred Years is the narration of Drake's attack and the exodus of
Ursula's great-great-grandparents; the first page of the novel is characterized by deceleration.

Frequency, Genette's third temporal category, is divided into three
classes—singulative, repetitive, and iterative. The singulative is a single
description of one event, such as the shooting death of José Arcadio (130).
The repetitive is the repeated narration of a single event (Aureliano's facing
the firing squad, for example, or his discovery of ice). The repetitive form

is often used to emphasize the importance of a particular episode and in *One Hundred Years* to underline the circular nature of the story by constituting an iconic diagram. (Mieke Bal in "Mise en abyme et iconicité" applies this term to a formal or stylistic aspect of the text that suggests an aspect of the fictitious world by resemblance.) The iterative is the single narration of several events treated as equivalent; it is frequently used to describe habitual behavior: "In the small separate room . . . he spoke to them about the wonders of the world" (24) refers to an act repeated many times.

Characterization on the level of text can be analyzed by identifying the various character indicators, which Rimmon-Kenan divides into two main categories (59): (1) Direct definition, in which the narrator explicitly gives us the essential character traits; this is the manner in which most characters in *One Hundred Years* are introduced. Ursula, for example, is defined as "[a]ctive, small, severe" (18) and José Arcadio Buendía as "the most enterprising man ever to be seen in the village" (18). (2) Indirect presentation, in which the narrator leaves the reader to infer the main character traits. Character indicators in this category include action, speech, external appearance (Ursula's "stiff, starched petticoats" [18] suggest a particular character trait), environment (Rebeca's gloomy and dilapidated house is an iconic diagram of its occupant), analogy between a proper name and a character (Fernanda del Carpio's surname suggests her quarrelsome nature [*carpir* = quarrel]; Amaranta's bitterness is indicated by her name [*amarga* = bitter]; Aureliano's name suggests his favorite pastime, modeling gold ornaments in the form of fish [*aurum* = gold]), analogous landscape (not pertinent in *One Hundred Years*), and analogy between characters (character indicators of Colonel Aureliano, for example, give us information about the other Aurelianos).

A useful concept for the analysis of character presentation is focalization (Genette, *Figures III* 206–23), which Rimmon-Kenan situates on the level of text. Not quite equivalent to Wayne Booth's point of view or mode of narrative presentation, Genette's focalization refers exclusively to the subject that sees, feels, or thinks—Rimmon-Kenan distinguishes between perceptual, psychological, and ideological aspects of focalization (77–82)—and narrative voice is relegated to a separate category. Genette makes an absolute distinction between who sees (the focalizer) and who speaks (the narrator), but point-of-view studies frequently take aspects of narrative voice into account. Even if it is sometimes difficult to make a practical distinction between focalization and narration, since the focalizer is a construct obtained by analyzing the positions adopted by the narrator or the characters, the distinction made by Genette remains pertinent. Genette divides focalization into three categories—external (the focalizer observes only what is directly perceptible, such as speech and action), internal (the focalizer reveals personal thoughts and feelings), and zero (an omniscient focalizer, identified with the undramatized narrator, has unlimited access to the characters' emotions). Mieke Bal has rightly criticized this heterogeneous tripartite division and has suggested a distinction between the subject and the object of focalization ("Narration"). Rimmon-Kenan redefines external focalization as that of the narrator as subject and internal focalization as that of a character as subject; she labels focalization of what is perceptible "focalization from without" and focalization of thoughts and feelings "focalization from within" (75). I prefer to maintain the equivalence between external-internal and focalization of what is perceptible-imperceptible and to distinguish between a dramatized focalizer and an undramatized focalizer. In *One Hundred Years* the main focalizer is undramatized and anonymous (like the narrator) and focalizes the characters externally and internally. The description of Ursula (18) is external; the narration of Aureliano's childhood memory of ice is internal (11), since it is imperceptible to a normal observer. *One Hundred Years* has no lengthy internal focalization, as the novel is more concerned with action than with psychological complexity. One trait of the main focalizer is the detached and apparently objective observation of supernatural events. What would have surprised and disconcerted the focalizer in a traditional fantastic story (ghosts, flying carpets, levitation) does not produce any response in the anonymous and dramatized focalizers of *One Hundred Years* (see 25, 38, 80, 85, 129, 137, 222–3, 259–60). This lack of response can also be analyzed on the level of enunciation.

The narrator of *One Hundred Years*, undramatized and anonymous, is labeled extradiegetic in Genette's typology (*Figures III* 238), since he or she is not represented as a character-narrator within the story (or diegesis) but functions as a first-level narrator of a story told retrospectively. The narrator is also heterodiegetic (*Figures III* 255–56), not participating in the story as a character. The narrator's degree of perceptibility ranges from maximum overtness to maximum covertness (Chatman 197–252); one can situate him or her near the pole of maximum overtness, according to Chatman's criteria of description of setting, identification of characters, temporal summary, definition of character, reports of what characters did not think or say, and commentary on the story (Rimmon-Kenan 96–100). This overtness corresponds to the preponderance of the purely diegetic, maximum presence of the narrator in telling and organizing the story, as opposed to the purely mimetic, maximum imitation of characters' speech (McHale 258–59). According to McHale's categories of speech representation, *One Hundred Years* is close to the pole of the purely diegetic on the following descending scale (Rimmon-Kenan 109–10):

1. Diegetic summary, report that a speech act has occurred: "Ursula Iguarán . . . was unable to dissuade him" (12).
2. Summary, less purely diegetic: "He . . . demonstrated to them, with theories that none of them could understand, the possibility of returning to where one had set out by consistently sailing east" (14).

3. Indirect content paraphrase or indirect discourse: "Other gypsies confirmed later on that Melquíades had in fact succumbed to the fever on the beach at Singapore and that his body had been thrown into the deepest part of the Java Sea" (25).
4. Indirect discourse, mimetic to some degree, in which some aspects of style are preserved: "According to what he himself said . . . death followed him everywhere, sniffing at the cuffs of his pants . . ." (15).
5. Free indirect discourse: Fernanda's diatribe (298–301).

Category 6 (direct discourse) accounts for a relatively small proportion of the novel. I could not find any examples of category 7 (free direct discourse, first-person interior monologue).

An analysis of enunciation reveals even more discursive complexity than is at first apparent. Particular discursive features characterize the speech of individual characters and their presentation by the narrator (Paraíso de Leal 209–10; most of the following examples are taken from this study). Melquíades's poetic speech, for example—"Things have a life of their own. . . . It's simply a matter of waking up their souls" (11)—is echoed by the narrator's style: "He wore a large black hat that looked like a raven with widespread wings, and a velvet vest across which the patina of the centuries had skated" (15). Ursula, by contrast, frequently uses colloquial expressions—"you should be worrying about your sons. . . . Look at the state they're in, running wild just like donkeys" (22)—as does the narrator when describing her: "Ursula and the children broke their backs in the garden" (14). The discursive features characterizing Melquíades's and Ursula's speech provide information on the subject of enunciation: Melquíades's poetic speech indicates his mystical attitude toward the world; Ursula's familiar and down-to-earth style reveals her attitude and approach to life. Paraíso de Leal also points out that the narrator's style vacillates, even within a single sentence, from poetic to comic, tragic, and familiar (210–12). The poetic description of Melquíades —"lighting up with his deep organ voice the darkest reaches of the imagination"—contrasts with the familiar and comic style of the rest of the sentence: "while down over his temples there flowed the grease that was being melted by the heat" (15). A Bakhtinian analysis of the various discourses in *One Hundred Years* and of the ubiquitous presence of the voice of the other (expressions and discursive patterns—identified with specific registers, levels of language, and stylistic contexts—that are consciously or unconsciously assimilated and integrated within one's speech) is particularly pertinent (Bakhtin, *Problems, Dialogic Imagination*). Bakhtin, in fact, considered the simultaneous presence of conflicting discourses (polyphony) the main characteristic of the modern novel. A character's speech is not seen as entirely unique and original but is situated within a complex, heterogeneous and contradictory ensemble of discourses characterizing a particular society at a given time. The character's speech can, therefore, be analyzed both from the perspective of enunciation (information on the subject's character and attitude toward the world, for example) and from the perspective of a more comprehensive discourse analysis, which goes beyond a strictly narratological approach. A detailed analysis of enunciation and discourse in general is not completely satisfactory when working with a translated version, but the examples I have given, as well as many others that can be found in a non-Spanish rendering of *One Hundred Years*, preserve the original style, especially in Rabassa's excellent translation.

A particularly interesting passage is Fernanda's diatribe (298–301). Introduced and occasionally interrupted by the narrator, her complaints are ironically mediated by an enunciator who does not share her opinion and whose poetic and humorous comparisons of her harangue to "an uncontained, unchained torrent that began one morning as the monotonous drone of a guitar" and "a buzzing that was by then more fluid and louder than the sound of the rain" prevent the reader from identifying with her position. The description of her litany as "implacable horsefly buzzing" reveals the narrator's attitude and trivializes the gravity of her accusations and laments. Rendered by means of free indirect discourse, her criticism of various family members and some aspects of her discourse are ironically juxtaposed with her dialogic quotation of the opinions of others. Her indignation at being called a pharisee and a church mouse appears especially comical, since she confirms the judgment of her relatives by condemning her husband for his idolatry, claiming that she bears her situation "with resignation because of the Holy Father" and because she is "God-fearing, obeying His laws and submissive to His wishes," considering her father "a fine Christian, a Knight of the Order of the Holy Sepulcher, those who receive direct from God the privilege of remaining intact in their graves," and lacing her diatribe with expressions such as "from the time God gave his morning sunlight until it was time to go to bed," "God have mercy," and "may she rest in peace." Her reference to "that peasant of an Amaranta . . . who thought that white wine was served in the daytime" and her pride at being "a lady of such lineage that she made the liver of presidents' wives quiver" reveal just as much about her character and cultural background as José Arcadio Segundo's description of her as "a stuck-up highlander."

This brief narratological exposition is anything but exhaustive, and additional narratological concepts and models can be found in the works referred to. But I have found that the preceding analytical tools work well in a classroom situation and provide a good introduction to the narratological approach.

CONTRIBUTORS AND SURVEY PARTICIPANTS

The editors are grateful to the teachers who participated in a survey in which they described their approaches to teaching *One Hundred Years of Solitude* and the materials they used in preparation. Their ideas helped organize and structure this volume.

Isabel Alvarez Borland, Coll. of the Holy Cross; Sandra M. Boschetto, Michigan Technological Univ.; Michael F. Capobianco, Saint John's Univ.; Amaryll Chanady, Univ. of Montreal; Gwendolyn Diaz, Saint Mary's Univ., San Antonio; Gary Eddy, Winona State Univ.; Arthur Efron, State Univ. of New York, Buffalo; Oscar Fernández, Univ. of Iowa, Emeritus; Hanna Geldrich-Leffman, Loyola Coll., Baltimore; Chester S. Halka, Randolph-Macon Woman's Coll.; Paul M. Hedeen, Univ. of Cincinnati; R. A. Kerr, Rollins Coll.; Naomi Lindstrom, Univ. of Texas, Austin; Kern L. Lunsford, Lynchburg Coll.; Walter D. Mignolo, Univ. of Michigan, Ann Arbor; Gabriela Mora, Rutgers Univ., New Brunswick; Mabel Moraña, Univ. of California, Santa Cruz; William A. Nericcio, Cornell Univ.; Teobaldo A. Noriega, Trent Univ.; Mary Rice, Coe Coll.; D. L. Shaw, Univ. of Virginia; Robert L. Sims, Virginia Commonwealth Univ.; María Elena de Valdés, Univ. of Toronto; Mario J. Valdés, Univ. of Toronto; A. M. Vazquez-Bigi, Univ. of Tennessee, Knoxville; Nancy Watanabe, Norman, Oklahoma; Raymond Leslie Williams, Univ. of Colorado, Boulder; Rose A. Zak, Boston Coll.; Lois Parkinson Zamora, Univ. of Houston, Houston.

WORKS CITED

Aaron, M. Audrey. "Remedios, la bella, and 'The Man in the Green Velvet Suit.' "
    Chasqui 9.2–3 (1980): 39–48.

Aguiar, Neuma. "Research Guidelines: How to Study Women's Work in Latin Amer-
    ica." *Women and Change in Latin America*. Ed. June Nash and Helen I. Safa.
    South Hadley: Bergin, 1986. 22–35.

Ahmad, Aijaz. "Jameson's Rhetoric of Otherness and the 'National Allegory.' " *Social
    Text* 17 (1987): 3–25.

Alazraki, Jaime. "New Fantastic Literature: A Structuralist Answer." *The Analysis
    of Literary Texts: Current Trends in Methodology*. Ed. R. D. Pope. Ypsilanti:
    Bilingual, 1980. 286–90.

Alter, Robert. *Partial Magic: The Novel as a Self-Conscious Genre*. Berkeley: U of
    California P, 1975.

Althusser, Louis. "Ideology and Ideological State Apparatuses (Notes towards an
    Investigation)." *Lenin and Philosophy and Other Essays*. Trans. Ben Brewster.
    New York: Monthly Review, 1971. 127–86.

Alvarez Gardeázabal, Gustavo. "Las formas de hacer el amor en *Cien años de so-
    ledad*." Porrata and Avendaño 39–64.

Arciniegas, Germán. *Latin America: A Cultural History*. Trans. Joan MacLean. New
    York: Knopf, 1968.

Asturias, Miguel Angel. "Introducción a la novela latinoamericana." *América, fábula
    de fábulas*. Caracas: Monte Avila, 1972. 141–49.

Bachelard, Gaston. *The Poetics of Space*. Trans. Maria Jolas. Boston: Beacon, 1969.

Bakhtin, Mikhail. *The Dialogic Imagination: Four Essays*. Ed. Michael Holquist.
    Trans. Caryl Emerson and Michael Holquist. Austin: Texas UP, 1981.

———. "Discourse in the Novel." *Dialogic Imagination* 259–422.

———. *Problems of Dostoevsky's Poetics*. Ann Arbor: Ardis, 1973.

Bal, Mieke. "Mise en abyme et iconicité." *Littérature* 30 (1978): 116–28.

———. "Narration et focalisation: Pour une théorie des instances du récit." *Poétique*
    8.1 (1977): 107–27.

Barnet, Miguel. *Biografía de un cimarrón*. Havana: Academia de Ciencias, 1966.

Barthes, Roland. "Introduction à l'analyse structurale des récits." *Communications*
    8 (1966): 1–27.

———. *S/Z*. Trans. Richard Miller. London: Hill, 1974.

Bell-Villada, Gene H. "Banana Strike and Military Massacre: *One Hundred Years
    of Solitude* and What Happened in 1928." *From Dante to García Márquez*.
    Ed. Gene H. Bell-Villada, Antonio Giménez, and George Pistorius. Williams-
    town: Williams Coll., 1987. 391–403.

Belsey, Catherine. *Critical Practice*. London: Methuen, 1980.

Benveniste, Emile. *Problems in General Linguistics.* Trans. Mary Elizabeth Meek. Coral Gables: U of Miami P, 1971.

Bergquist, Charles W. *Coffee and Conflict in Colombia, 1886–1910.* Durham: Duke UP, 1986.

Bessière, Irène. *Le récit fantastique: La poétique de l'incertain.* Paris: Larousse, 1974.

Bethell, Leslie, ed. *The Cambridge History of Latin America.* 5 vols. Cambridge: Cambridge UP, 1984–86.

Billeter, Erika, ed. *Images of Mexico: The Contribution of Mexico to Twentieth Century Art.* Exhibition catalog. Dallas: Dallas Museum of Art, 1988.

Blanco Aguinaga, Carlos. "Sobre la lluvia y la historia en las ficciones de García Márquez." *De mitólogos y novelistas.* Ed. Juan Bautista Avalle-Arce. Madrid: Ediciones Turner, 1975. 27–50.

Booth, Wayne. *The Rhetoric of Fiction.* Chicago: U of Chicago P, 1961.

Borges, Jorge Luis. *La literatura fantástica.* Buenos Aires: Ediciones Olivetti, 1967.

Braudel, Fernand. *L'identité de la France.* Paris: Arthaud-Flammarion, 1986.

Bremond, Claude. *Logique du récit.* Paris: Seuil, 1973.

Bryan, Avril. "Myth and Superstition in *Cien años de soledad.*" *Myth and Superstition in Spanish-Caribbean Literature.* Proc. of Fifth Conference of Hispanists. Mona: U of West Indies, 1982. 68–84.

———. "Virginity: Contrasting Views in the Works of Miguel de Unamuno and Gabriel García Márquez." *La mujer en la literatura caribeña.* Proc. of Sixth Conference of Hispanists. St. Augustine: U of West Indies, [1985?]. 168–84.

Burns, Graham. "García Márquez and the Idea of Solitude." *Critical Review* [Canberra, Austral.] 27 (1985): 18–33.

Bushnell, David. "The Independence of Spanish South America." Bethell 3: 95–156.

Caicedo Jurado, Cecilia. "El machismo en la narrativa de Gabriel García Márquez." *Meridiano* [Pasto, Col.] 6.17 (1973): 66–76.

Calasans Rodríguez, Selma. "*Cien años de soledad* y las crónicas de la conquista." *Revista de la Universidad de México* 38.23 (1983): 13–16.

Campbell, Joseph. *The Hero With a Thousand Faces.* Princeton: Princeton UP, 1973.

Carpentier, Alejo. "Lo barroco y lo real maravilloso." *La novela latinoamericana en vísperas de un nuevo siglo.* México: Siglo Veintiuno Editores, 1981. 111–35.

———. "De lo real maravilloso americano." *Tientos y diferencias.* Montevideo: Arca, 1967. 103–21.

———. "Prólogo." *El reino de este mundo.* México: Ediapsa, 1949.

Carrillo, Germán Darío. "Mito bíblico y experiencia humana en *Cien años de soledad.*" Porrata and Avendaño 79–100.

———. *La narrativa de Gabriel García Márquez.* Madrid: Castalia, 1975.

Castro-Klaren, Sara. "The Space of Solitude in *Cien años de soledad.*" *Working Paper* 18. Washington: Wilson Center, 1978.

Cavallari, Héctor Mario. "Ficción, testimonio, representación." *Semiosis: Seminario de semiótica, teoría, análisis* [Xalapa, Mex.] 14–15 (1985): 110–22.

Cepeda Samudio, Alvaro. *La casa grande.* 2nd ed. Preface Gabriel García Márquez. Bogotá: Plaza y Janés, 1967.

Chaney, Elsa M. *Women of the World: Latin America and the Caribbean.* Washington: U.S. Dept. of Commerce, Bureau of the Census, 1984.

Chatman, Seymour. *Story and Discourse.* Ithaca: Cornell UP, 1978.

Chiampi, Irlemar. *O realismo maravilloso: Forma e ideologia no romance hispano-americano.* Sao Paolo: Editora Perspectiva, 1980.

Collver, Andrew. *Birth Rates in Latin America.* Berkeley: U of California P, 1965.

Commission on the Status of Women. *Report of the Special Committee for Studies and Recommendations of the InterAmerican Commission of Women for the World Congress of International Women's Year.* Washington: Organization of American States, 1975.

Connell, R. W. *Which Way Is Up? Essays on Sex, Class and Culture.* Sidney: Allen, 1983.

Cornejo Polar, Antonio. "El indigenismo y las literaturas heterogéneas: Su doble estatuto socio-cultural." *Revista de crítica literaria latinoamericana* [Lima] 4.7–8 (1978): 7–21.

Corvalán, Octavio. "Faulkner y García Márquez: Una aproximacíon." *Revista Sur* 349 (1981): 71–88.

Cosse, Rómulo. "*Cien años de soledad:* Ideología y plasmación narrativa." Oyarzún and Megenney 75–87.

Cueva, Agustín. "Para una interpretación sociológica de *Cien años de soledad.*" *Revista chilena de literatura* 5–6 (1972): 151–70.

Culler, Jonathan. *The Pursuit of Signs: Semiotics, Literature, Deconstruction.* London: Routledge, 1981.

Day, Holliday T., and Hollister Sturges, eds. *Art of the Fantastic: Latin America, 1920–1987.* Exhibition catalog. Indianapolis: Indianapolis Museum of Art, 1987.

Deas, Malcolm. "Colombia: 1880–1930." Bethell 5: 644–63.

———. "Venezuela, Colombia and Ecuador: The First Half-Century of Independence." Bethell 3: 507–38.

De Costa, Rene. *The Poetry of Pablo Neruda.* Cambridge: Harvard UP, 1979.

Dessau, Adalbert. "El tema de la soledad en las novelas de Gabriel García Márquez." *El ensayo y la crítica literaria en Iberoamérica.* Memoria del XIV Congreso Internacional de Literatura Iberoamericana. Ed. Kurt L. Levy and Keith Ellis. Toronto: U of Toronto, 1970. 209–14.

Dilmore, Gene. "*One Hundred Years of Solitude:* Some Translation Corrections." *Journal of Modern Literature* 11 (1984): 311–14.

Dinnerstein, Dorothy. *The Mermaid and the Minotaur: Sexual Arrangements and Human Malaise.* New York: Harper, 1976.

Di Pietro, Robert J. *Strategic Interaction: Learning Languages through Scenarios.* Cambridge: Cambridge UP, 1987.

Di Virgilio, Paul. "Literary Negativity in 'Shifting-Out': Aquin, Faulkner, and García Márquez." Valdés 107–11.

Dix, Robert H. *Colombia: The Political Dimensions of Change.* New Haven: Yale UP, 1967.

D'Onofrio-Flores, Pamela M. "Technology, Economic Development and the Division of Labour by Sex." *Scientific and Technological Change and the Role of Women in Development.* Boulder: United Nations Inst. for Training and Research, 1982. 13–28.

Donoso, José. *Casa de campo.* Barcelona: Seix Barral, 1978.

Dreifus, Claudia. "Interview with Gabriel García Márquez." *Playboy* Feb. 1983: 65–77, 172–78.

Eagleton, Terry. *Criticism and Ideology: A Study in Marxist Literary Theory.* London: New Left, 1976.

Earle, Peter, ed. *Gabriel García Márquez: El escritor y la crítica.* Madrid: Taurus, 1981.

Eaves, Arthur J. "Tiempo y significación en *Cien años de soledad.*" *En el punto de mira: Gabriel García Márquez.* Ed. Ana María Hernández de López. Madrid: Pliegos, 1985. 105–13.

Eliade, Mircea. *Rites and Symbols of Initiation: The Mysteries of Birth and Rebirth.* Trans. Willard R. Trask. New York: Harper, 1958.

Elu de Leñero, María del Carmen. "Woman's Work and Fertility." *Sex and Class in Latin America: Women's Perspectives on Politics, Economics and the Family.* Ed. June Nash and Helen Icken Saba. Brooklyn: Bergin, 1980. 46–68.

Farías, Víctor. *Los manuscritos de Melquíades:* Cien años de soledad: *Burguesía latinoamericana y dialéctica de la reproducción ampliada de negación.* Frankfurt: Verlag Klaus Dieter Vervuert, 1981.

Faris, Wendy B. "Icy Solitude: Magic and Violence in Macondo and San Lorenzo." *Gabriel García Márquez,* Special issue of *Latin American Literary Review* 13.25 (1985): 44–54.

———. "Marking Space, Charting Time: Text and Time in Faulkner's 'The Bear' and Carpentier's *Los pasos perdidos.*" Pérez Firmat 243–65.

Fau, Margaret Eustella. *Gabriel García Márquez: An Annotated Bibliography, 1947–1979.* Westport: Greenwood, 1980.

Fau, Margaret Eustella, and Nelly Sfeir de González. *Bibliographical Guide to Gabriel García Márquez, 1979–1985.* Westport: Greenwood, 1986.

Fernández, Jesse. "La ética del trabajo y la acumulación de la riqueza en *Cien años de soledad.*" *Hispamérica: Revista de literatura* 13.37 (1984): 73–79.

Fernández, Margarita. "El personaje femenino en *Cien años de soledad.*" *Revista del Convenio Andrés Bello* [Bogotá] (1981): 59–81.

Fernández-Braso, Miguel. *Gabriel García Márquez.* Madrid: Editorial Azur, 1969.

———. *La soledad de Gabriel García Márquez: Una conversación infinita.* Barcelona: Planeta, 1972.

Five Studies on the Situation of Women in Latin America. Santiago, Chile: United Nations, 1983.

Fluharty, Vernon L. *Dance of the Millions: Military Rule and the Social Revolution in Colombia 1930–1956.* Pittsburgh: U of Pittsburgh P, 1957.

Foster, David William. "García Márquez and Solitude." *Americas* [Washington] 21 (1969): 36–41.

Foucault, Michel. *The Order of Things: An Archeology of the Human Sciences.* New York: Pantheon, 1970.

Fuentes, Carlos. "García Márquez: La segunda lectura." *La nueva novela hispanoamericana.* México: Mortiz, 1969. 58–67.

"Fuentes to Christopher Sharp." W. Supp. to *Women's Wear Daily* 29 Oct. 1977.

Gabriel García Márquez: La magia de lo real. Dir. Ana Cristiana Navarro. Films for the Humanities, 1981. 60 mins.

Gaitán, Jorge Eliécer. *Los mejores discursos 1919–48.* Ed. Jorge Villaveces. 2nd ed. Bogotá: Editorial Jorvi, 1968.

Galeano, Eduardo. *Open Veins of Latin America: Five Centuries of the Pillage of a Continent.* Trans. Cedric Belfrage. New York: Monthly Review, 1973.

Galloway Young, Katharine. *Taleworlds and Storyrealms: The Phenomenology of Narrative.* Dordrecht: Nijhoff, 1987.

García Márquez, Gabriel. *Cien años de soledad.* Buenos Aires: Editorial Sudamericana, 1967.

———. *Cien años de soledad.* Ed. Jacques Joset. Madrid: Ediciones Cátedra, 1987.

———. *Cien años de soledad.* México: Editorial Diana, 1988.

———. *Cien años de soledad* (fragment). Recording. Read by García Márquez. Mexico, Universidad Nacional Autónoma de México, 1967.

———. *Eréndira.* Film. Dir. Ruy Guerra. Spanish-Venezuelan co-production. 1983.

———. *La increíble y triste historia de la cándida Eréndira y de su abuela desalmada.* Buenos Aires: Editorial Sudamericana, 1972.

———. *El olor de la guayaba: Conversaciones con Plinio Apuleyo Mendoza.* Barcelona: Bruguera, 1983.

———. *One Hundred Years of Solitude.* Trans. Gregory Rabassa. New York: Harper, 1970.

———. *One Hundred Years of Solitude.* Trans. Gregory Rabassa. 1970. New York: Avon; London: Picador, 1972.

———. "Un señor muy viejo con unas alas enormes." *Todos los cuentos de Gabriel García Márquez.* Barcelona: Plaza y Janés, 1975. 213–20.

———. "The Solitude of Latin America: Nobel Address 1982." Trans. Richard Cardwell. McGuirk and Cardwell 207–11.

García Márquez, Gabriel, and Mario Vargas Llosa. *La novela en América Latina: Diálogo.* Lima: Carlos Milla Batres, 1968.

Garvey, James. "Characterization in Narrative." *Poetics* 7 (1978): 63–78.

Geertz, Clifford. "From the 'Native's' Point of View: On the Nature of Anthropological Understanding." *Bulletin of the American Academy of Arts and Sciences* 28.1 (1974). Rpt. in *Local Knowledge: Further Essays in Interpretive Anthropology.* Ed. Geertz. New York: Basic, 1983. 55–72.

Genette, Gérard. *Figures of Literary Discourse.* Trans. Alan Sheridan. New York: Columbia UP, 1982.

————. *Figures III*. Paris: Seuil, 1972. Trans. as *Narrative Discourse: An Essay in Method*. Trans. Jane E. Lewin. Ithaca: Cornell UP, 1980.

Giacoman, Helmy F., ed. *Homenaje a Gabriel García Márquez: Variaciones interpretativas en torno a su obra*. New York: Las Américas, 1972.

Gibson, William Marion. *The Constitutions of Colombia*. Durham: Duke UP, 1948.

Gissi Bustos, Jorge. "Mitología sobre la mujer." *La mujer en América Latina*. Ed. María del Carmen Elu de Leñero. Vol. 1. México: SepSetentas, 1975. 85–107. Rpt. as "Mythology about Women." Elu de Leñero 30–45.

Glade, William. "Latin America and the International Economy, 1870–1914." Bethell 4: 1–56.

González, Anibal. "Translation and Genealogy: *One Hundred Years of Solitude*." McGuirk and Cardwell 65–79.

González Echevarría, Roberto. "*Cien años de soledad*: The Novel as Myth and Archive." *Modern Language Notes* 99.2 (1984): 358–80.

————. "With Borges in Macondo." *Diacritics* 2.1 (1972): 57–60.

Gould, Eric. *Mythical Intentions in Modern Literature*. Princeton: Princeton UP, 1981.

Greimas, A. J. *Structural Semantics*. Trans. Danielle McDowell. Lincoln: U of Nebraska P, 1983.

Griffin, Clive. "The Humour of *One Hundred Years of Solitude*." McGuirk and Cardwell 81–94.

Guerin, Wilfred L., Earle Labor, Lee Morgan, and John R. Willingham. *A Handbook of Critical Approaches to Literature*. New York: Harper, 1979.

Guerra, José Joaquín. *Estudio sobre los concordatos celebrados entre su Santidad León XIII y el gobierno de Colombia en los años 1887 y 1892*. Bogotá, 1895.

Guibert, Rita. *Seven Voices: Seven Latin American Writers Talk to Rita Guibert*. Trans. Frances Partridge. New York: Knopf, 1973. 303–37.

Gullón, Ricardo. "Gabriel García Márquez and the Lost Art of Storytelling." *Diacritics* 1.1 (1971): 27–32.

Guzmán, Jorge. "*Cien años de soledad*: En vez de dioses, el español latinoamericano." *Diferencias latinoamericanas*. Santiago, Chile: Ediciones del Centro de Estudios Humanísticos, Universidad de Chile, 1984. 79–127.

Halka, Chester S. *Melquíades, Alchemy and Narrative Theory: The Quest for Gold in Cien años de soledad*. Troy: International, 1981.

————. "Perspectivismo en *Don Quijote* y *Cien años de soledad*: Una comparación." *Hispanófila* 89 (1987): 21–38.

Hall, Michael M., and Hobart A. Spalding, Jr. "The Urban Working Class and Early Latin American Labour Movements, 1880–1930." Bethell 4: 325–66.

Halperín Donghi, Tulio. *Historia contemporánea de América Latina*. Madrid: Editorial Alianza, 1983.

Harkess, Shirley J. "The Pursuit of an Ideal: Migration, Social Class, and Woman's Roles in Bogotá, Colombia." *Female and Male in Latin America: Essays*. Ed. Ann Pescatello. Pittsburgh: U of Pittsburgh P, 1973. 231–54.

Hart, Stephen. "Magical Realism in Gabriel García Márquez's *Cien años de soledad*." *INTI: Revista de literatura hispánica* 16–17 (1982–83): 37–52.

Hayles, N. Katherine. "Chaos in Contemporary Literature and Science: Local Sites and Global Systems." Sixteenth Annual Twentieth Century Literature Conference (Literature and Science). 25–27 Feb. 1988.

Hazera, Lydia D. "Estudio sinóptico de las personalidades femeninas." Porrata and Avendaño 151–69.

Hedeen, Paul M. "Gabriel García Márquez's Dialectic of Solitude." *Southwest Review* 68.4 (1983): 350–64.

Hudson, Wilson M. "Jung on Myth and the Mythic." *The Sunny Slopes of Long Ago*. Ed. Wilson M. Hudson and Allen Maxwell. Dallas: Southern Methodist UP, 1966. 181–97.

Iannone, A. Pablo. *Contemporary Moral Controversies in Technology*. New York: Oxford UP, 1987.

Incledon, John. "Writing and Incest in *One Hundred Years of Solitude*." Shaw and Vera-Godwin 51–64.

Jameson, Fredric. "Magical Narratives: Romance as Genre." *New Literary History* 7.1 (1975): 135–73.

———. *Marxism and Form: Twentieth Century Dialectical Theories of Literature*. Princeton: Princeton UP, 1971.

———. "Third World Literature in the Era of Multinational Capitalism." *Social Text* 15 (1986): 65–88.

Janes, Regina. *Gabriel García Márquez: Revolution in Wonderland*. Columbia: U of Missouri P, 1981.

———. "Liberals, Conservatives, and Bananas: Colombian Politics in the Fiction of Gabriel García Márquez." *Hispanófila* 82 (1984): 79–102.

Jara, René, and Jaime Mejía Duque. *Las claves del mito en García Márquez*. Valparaiso: Ediciones Universitarias de Valparaiso, 1972.

Jaramillo Uribe, Jaime. *El pensamiento colombiano en el siglo XIX*. Bogotá: Editorial Temis, 1964.

Jelinski, J. B. "Memory and the Remembered Structure of *Cien años de soledad*— García Márquez." *Revista de estudios hispánicos* 18.3 (1984): 323–33.

Jitrik, Noé. "La perifrástica productiva en *Cien años de soledad*." *Melanges à la mémoire d'André Joucla-Ruau*. Vol. 2. Aix-en-Provence: Université de Provence, 1978. 813–31.

Jung, Carl G. "Individual Dream Symbolism in Relation to Alchemy." *The Portable Jung*. Ed. Joseph Campbell. New York: Penguin, 1971. 323–455.

———. "Psychological Aspects of the Mother Archetype." *Four Archetypes*. Trans. R. F. C. Hull. Princeton: Princeton UP, 1954. 75–110.

———. "The Relations between the Ego and the Unconscious." *The Portable Jung*. Ed. Joseph Campbell. New York: Penguin, 1971. 70–138.

Kappeler, Susanne. "Voices of Patriarchy: Gabriel García Márquez's *One Hundred Years of Solitude*." *Teaching the Text*. Ed. Kappeler and Norman Bryson. London: Routledge, 1983. 148–63.

Kennedy, Alan. "Márquez: Resistance, Rebellion and Reading." *García Márquez and Latin America*. Ed. Alok Bhalla. New York: Envoy, 1987. 43–67.

Kepner, Charles David. *The Banana Empire*. New York: Vanguard, 1935.

Kerbrat-Orecchioni, Catherine. *L'enonciation: De la subjectivité dans le langage*. Paris: Armand Colin, 1980.

Knaster, Meri. *Women in Spanish America: An Annotated Bibliography from Pre-Conquest to Contemporary Times*. Boston: Hall, 1977.

Kulin, Katalin. *Creación mítica en la obra de García Márquez*. Budapest: Akadémiai Kiadó, 1980.

Kutzinski, Vera M. "The Logic of Wings: Gabriel García Márquez and Afro-American Literature." *Latin American Literary Review* 13.25 (1985): 133–46.

Lacan, Jacques. *The Four Fundamental Concepts of Psycho-Analysis*. Ed. Jacques-Alain Miller. Trans. Alan Sheridan. New York: Norton, 1978.

Laclau, Ernesto. *Practice and Ideology in Marxist Theory*. London: Verso, 1979.

Laclau, Ernesto, and Chantal Mouffe. *Hegemony and Socialist Strategy towards a Radical Democratic Politics*. Trans. Winston Moore and Paul Cammack. London: Verso, 1985.

Lester, Nancy. "A General View of Faulkner's Influence on Gabriel García Márquez." *Chu-Shikoku Studies in American Literature* [Hiroshima] 21 (1985): 1–11.

Levine, Suzanne Jill. *El espejo hablado: Un estudio de* Cien años de soledad. Caracas: Monte Avila, 1975.

Lichtblau, Myron I. "In Search of the Stylistic Key in *Cien años de soledad*." Oyarzún and Megenney 103–12.

López-Capestany, Pablo. "Gabriel García Márquez y la soledad." *Cuadernos hispanoamericanos* [Madrid] 297 (1975): 613–23.

Lotman, Juri. "On the Metalanguage of a Typological Description of Culture." *Semiótica* 14.2 (1975): 97–123.

Lowe, Elizabeth. "Visions of Violence: From Faulkner to the Contemporary City Fiction of Brazil and Colombia." Valdés 14–19.

Ludmer, Josefina. Cien años de soledad: *Una interpretación*. Buenos Aires: Tiempo Contemporáneo, 1972.

Lynch, John. "The Catholic Church in Latin America, 1830–1930." Bethell 4: 527–96.

Macherey, Pierre. *A Theory of Literary Production*. Trans. Geoffrey Wall. London: Routledge, 1978.

Maldonado-Denis, Manuel. *La violencia en la obra de García Márquez*. Bogotá: Ediciones Sudamericanas, 1977.

Maranda, Pierre. "Cendrillon: Théories des graphes et des ensembles." *Sémiotique narrative et textuelle*. Ed. Claude Chabrol. Paris: Larousse, 1973. 122–36.

Marcuse, Herbert. *One Dimensional Man: Studies in the Ideology of Advanced Industrial Society*. Boston: Beacon, 1966.

Marroquín, Lorenzo. *Las cosas en su punto: Ojeada sobre la situación de la iglesia en Colombia*. Bogotá, 1898.

Martin, Gerald. "On 'Magical' and Social Realism in García Márquez." McGuirk and Cardwell 95–116.

Maturo, Gabriela. *Claves simbólicas de García Márquez*. Buenos Aires: García Cambeiro, 1977.

Maupassant, Guy de. "Le fantastique." *Oeuvres completes*. Vol. 16. Paris: L'Edition d'Art, 1968–73. 141–43.

McGowan, John P. "*A la recherche du temps perdu* in *One Hundred Years of Solitude*." *Modern Fiction Studies* 28.4 (1982–83): 557–67.

McGreevey, William Paul. *An Economic History of Colombia: 1845–1930*. Cambridge: Cambridge UP, 1971.

McGuirk, Bernard, and Richard Cardwell, eds. *Gabriel García Márquez: New Readings*. Cambridge: Cambridge UP, 1987.

McHale, Brian. "Free Indirect Discourse: A Survey of Recent Accounts." *Poetics and Theory of Literature* 3 (1978): 249–87.

McMurray, George R. "*The Aleph* and *One Hundred Years of Solitude*: Two Microcosmic Worlds." Rossman and Miller 55–64.

———. *Gabriel García Márquez*. New York: Unger, 1977.

McNerney, Kathleen, and John Martin. "Alchemy in *Cien años de soledad*." Spec. medieval issue of *West Virginia University Philological Papers* 27 (1981): 106–12.

Mead, Robert G. "Aspectos del espacio y el tiempo en *La casa verde* y *Cien años de soledad*." *Cuadernos americanos* [Mex.] 179.6 (1971): 240–44.

Meier, Hugo. "Technology and Democracy, 1800–1860." *Mississippi Valley Historical Review* 43 (1957): 618–40.

Mena, Lucila Inés. "Bibliografía anotada sobre el ciclo de la violencia en la literatura colombiana." *Latin American Research Review* 13.3 (1978): 95–107.

———. "*Cien años de soledad*: Novela de 'la violencia.' " *Hispamérica* 5.1 (1976): 3–23.

———. *La función de la historia en* Cien años de soledad. Barcelona: Plaza y Janés, 1979.

———. "La huelga de la compañía bananera como expresión de lo real maravilloso americano en *Cien años de soledad*." *Bulletin hispanique* 74.3–4 (1972): 379–405.

Menchú, Rigoberta. *I . . . Rigoberta Menchú: An Indian Woman in Guatemala*. Ed. Elizabeth Burgos-Debray. Trans. Ann Wright. London: Verso, 1984.

Menton, Seymour. *Magic Realism Rediscovered: 1918–1981*. Philadelphia: Art Alliance, 1983.

Mercado Cardona, Homero. *Macondo: Una realidad llamada ficción*. Barranquilla, Col.: Ediciones Universidad del Atlántico, 1971.

Merrel, Floyd. "The Ideal World in Search of Its Reference: An Inquiry into the Underlying Nature of Magical Realism." *Chasqui* 4.2 (1975): 5–17.

Meyers, Kate Beaird. "The Coded Beginning: Meaning in the First Sentence of *Cien años de soledad*." *Confluencia: Revista hispánica de cultura y literatura* 6.2 (1986): 33–38.

Mignolo, Walter D. "Dominios borrosos y dominios teóricos: Ensayo de elucidación conceptual." *Filología* 20.1 (1985): 21–40.

———. "Ficcionalización del discurso historiográfico." Ed. Saúl Sosnowski. *Augusto Roa Bastos y la producción cultural americana*. Buenos Aires: Ediciones de la Flor, 1986. 197–210.

———. *Teoría del texto e interpretación de textos*. México: Universidad Nacional Autónoma de México, 1986.

Mink, Louis O. *Historical Understanding*. Ithaca: Cornell UP, 1987.

Minta, Stephen. *Gabriel García Márquez, Writer of Colombia*. New York: Harper; London: Cape, 1987.

Montes-Huidobro, Matías. "From Hitchcock to García Márquez." Shaw and Vera-Godwin 91–104.

Mottram, Eric. "Existential and Political Controls in the Fiction of Gabriel García Márquez." *García Márquez and Latin America*. Ed. Alok Bhalla. New York: Envoy, 1987. 6–28.

Neumann, Erich. *The Great Mother*. Trans. Ralph Manheim. Princeton: Princeton UP, 1963.

———. *The Origins and History of Consciousness*. Trans. R. F. C. Hull. 2 vols. New York: Harper, 1962.

Neves, Eugenia. "Variaciones sobre Gabriel García Márquez: Sus novelas, ficción y realidad en América Latina." *Araucaria de Chile* 21 (1983): 131–40.

Oberhelman, Harley D. *The Presence of Faulkner in the Writings of García Márquez*. Lubbock: Texas Tech UP, 1980.

Oquist, Paul H. *Violence, Conflict and Politics in Colombia*. New York: Academic, 1980.

Ortega, Julio. "Canje, intercambio y valor: La economía signica en *Cien años de soledad*." *Discurso literario: Revista de temas hispánicos* 4.2 (1987): 633–45.

———, ed. *Gabriel García Márquez and the Powers of Fiction*. Austin: U of Texas P, 1988.

———. "Latin American Literature Facing the Eighties." *New Orleans Review* 7.3 (1980): 294–96.

Ortega y Gasset, José. *Ideas sobre la novela (1924–1925)*. Madrid: Espasa Calpe, 1964.

Osuña, Yolanda. "El incesto como línea accional en *Cien años de soledad*." *Tres ensayos de análisis literario*. Mérida: Gráficos Universitarios, 1980. 13–54.

Oxford English Dictionary. 2nd ed.

Oyarzún, Kemy, and William W. Megenney. *Essays on Gabriel García Márquez*. Riverside: Latin American Studies Program, U of California, 1984.

Palencia-Roth, Michael. *Gabriel García Márquez: La línea, el círculo y las metamorfosis del mito*. Madrid: Gredos, 1983.

Paraíso de Leal, Isabel. "Un lenguaje poético y apresurado: *Cien años de soledad*." Porrata and Avendaño 207–38.

Paz, Octavio. *The Labyrinth of Solitude: Life and Thought in Mexico*. 1961. Trans. Lysander Kemp. New York: Grove, 1985.

Peden, Margaret Sayers. "Las buenas y las malas mujeres de Macondo." Porrata and Avendaño 313–28.

Penuel, Arnold M. "Death and the Maiden Demythologization of Virginity in García Márquez's *Cien años de soledad*." *Hispania* 66.4 (1983): 552–60.

Pérez Firmat, Gustavo, ed. *Do the Americas Have a Common Literature?* Durham: Duke UP, 1990.

Piglia, Ricardo. *Respiración artificial*. Buenos Aires: Pomaire, 1980.

Pinard, Mary C. "Time in and out of Solitude in *One Hundred Years of Solitude*." Shaw and Vera-Godwin 65–72.

Porrata, Francisco E. "La novela y sus componentes: La voz narrativa en *Cien años de soledad*." Porrata and Avendaño 7–38.

Porrata, Francisco E., and Fausto Avendaño, eds. *Explicación de* Cien años de soledad. San José, Costa Rica: Editorial Texto, 1976.

Porter, Lawrence M. "The Political Function of Fantasy in García Márquez." *Centennial Review* 30.2 (1986): 196–207.

Poulet, Georges. *Studies in Human Time*. Trans. Elliott Coleman. Baltimore: Johns Hopkins UP, 1956.

Prince, Gerald. *A Grammar of Stories*. The Hague: Mouton, 1973.

Propp, Vladimir. *Morphology of the Folktale*. Austin: U of Texas P, 1968.

Rabinowitz, Peter J. *Before Reading: Narrative Conventions and the Politics of Interpretation*. Ithaca: Cornell UP, 1987.

Rama, Angel. "De Gabriel García Márquez a Plinio Apuleyo Mendoza." *Eco* [Bogotá] 32/6.198 (1978), 33/1–2.199–200 (1978): 837–59.

———. "Literatura y cultura en América Latina." *Revista de critica literaria latinoamericana* [Lima] 9.18 (1983): 7–35.

——— "Un novelista de la violencia." *Nueve asedios a García Márquez*. Ed. Pedro Lastra. Santiago, Chile: Editorial Universitaria, 1971. 106–25.

Ramkrishnan, E. V. "The Novel of Memory and the Third World Reality: Gabriel Márquez and Chinua Achebe." *Indian Readings in Commonwealth Literature*. Ed. G. S. Amur et al. New York: Sterling, 1985. 124–31.

Ramos Escobar, José Luis. "Desde Yoknapatawpha a Macondo: Un estudio comparado de William Faulkner y Gabriel García Márquez." *En el punto de mira: Gabriel García Márquez*. Ed. Ana María Hernández de López. Madrid: Pliegos, 1985. 287–313.

Ricoeur, Paul. "The Model of the Text: Meaningful Actions Considered as a Text." *Social Research* 38 (1971): 529–62.

———. *Time and Narrative*. 3 vols. Chicago: U of Chicago P, 1984–87.

Rimmon-Kenan, Shlomith. *Narrative Fiction: Contemporary Poetics*. London: Methuen, 1983.

Rodríguez, Ileana. "Principios estructurales y visión estructural en *Cien años de soledad*." *Revista de crítica literaria latinoamericana* 9.5 (1979): 79–97.

Rodríguez-Luis, Julio. "García Márquez: Compromiso y alienación." *La literatura hispanoamericana entre compromiso y experimento*. Madrid: Espiral-Fundamentos, 1984. 201–31.

Rodríguez Monegal, Emir. "Realismo mágico versus literatura fantástica: Un diálogo de sordos." *Otros mundos otros fuegos: Fantasía y realismo mágico en Iber-*

oamérica. Ed. Donald A. Yates. East Lansing: Michigan State U, 1975. 25–37.

Rojas, Mario. "Tipología del discurso del personaje en el texto." *Dispositio: Revista hispánica de semiótica literaria* 5–6.15–16 (1980–81): 19–55.

Rossman, Charles, and Yvette E. Miller, eds. *Gabriel García Márquez*. Spec. issue of *Latin American Literary Review* 13.25 (1985): 7–160.

Ruthven, K. K. *Myth*. New York: Methuen, 1976.

Safford, Frank. *The Ideal of the Practical: Colombia's Struggle to Form a Technical Elite*. Austin: U of Texas P, 1983.

———. "Politics, Ideology and Society in Post-Independence Spanish America." Bethell 3: 347–421.

Said, Edward. *Covering Islam*. New York: Pantheon, 1981.

———. *Orientalism*. New York: Pantheon, 1978.

Saine, Ute M. "Einstein and Musil in Macondo: *One Hundred Years of Solitude* and the Theory of Relativity." Oyarzún and Megenney 36–50.

Sainte-Marie, A. *Etude des personnages feminins de* Cien años de soledad *de Gabriel García Márquez*. Toulouse–Le Mirail: Université de Toulouse–Le Mirail, 1983.

Saldívar, José David. "Ideology and Deconstruction in Macondo." Rossman and Miller 29–43.

Sangari, Kumkum. "The Politics of the Possible." *Cultural Critique* 7 (1987): 157–86.

Sarmiento, Domingo F. *Life in the Argentine Republic in the Days of the Tyrants: Or, Civilization and Barbarism*. 1868. New York: Macmillan, 1974.

Scholes, Robert. *Textual Power: Literary Theory and the Teaching of English*. New Haven: Yale UP, 1985.

Scott, Nina M. "Inter-American Literature: An Antidote to the Arrogance of Culture." *College English* 41.6 (1980): 635–64.

Segre, Cesare. "Il tempo curvo di Gabriel García Márquez." *I segni e la critica*. Torino: Einaudi, 1969. 252–95.

Semprún Donahue, Moraima. "Una interpretación de símbolos de García Márquez: El oro y lo amarillo." *Cuadernos americanos* [Mex.] 205.2 (1976): 226–39.

Serra, Edelweis. "Narrema e isotopía en *Cien años de soledad* de Gabriel García Márquez." *El mensaje literario: Estudios estilísticos y semiológicos*. Rosario: Universidad Nacional de Rosario, 1979. 119–41.

Sexson, Michael. "Postmodern Paradigms: The Enchantment of Realism in the Fiction of Italo Calvino and Gabriel García Márquez." *Journal of Social and Biological Structures* 6.2 (1983): 115–21.

Shaw, Bradley A., and N. Vera-Godwin, eds. *Critical Perspectives on Gabriel García Márquez*. Lincoln: U of Nebraska P, 1986.

Siemens, William W. "Tiempo, entropía y la estructura de *Cien años de soledad*." Porrata and Avendaño 359–71.

Sims, Robert L. "The Banana Massacre in *Cien años de soledad*: A Micro-structural Example of Myth, History and Bricolage." *Chasqui* 8.3 (1979): 3–23.

―――. "Claude Simon and Gabriel García Márquez: The Conflicts between *histoire-Histoire* and *historia-Historia.*" *Papers on Romance Literary Relations.* Ed. Cyrus Decoster. Evanston: Northwestern U, 1975. 1–22.

―――. *The Evolution of Myth in Gabriel García Márquez: From* La hojarasca *to* Cien años de soledad. Miami: Universal, 1981.

―――. "El laboratorio periodístico de García Márquez: Lo carnavalesco y la creación del espacio novelístico." *Revista iberoamericana* 52.137 (1986): 979–89.

Snell, Susan. "William Faulkner, un guía sureño a la ficción de García Márquez." *En el punto de mira: García Márquez.* Ed. Ana María Hernández de López. Madrid: Pliegos, 1985. 315–26.

Spivak, Gayatri Chakravorty. *In Other Worlds: Essays in Cultural Politics.* London: Methuen, 1987.

Taylor, Anna Marie. "*Cien años de soledad*: History and the Novel. *Latin American Perspectives* 2.3 (1975): 96–112.

Thompson, John B. *Studies in the Theory of Ideology.* Cambridge: Polity, 1984.

Thorp, Rosemary. "Latin America and the International Economy from the First World War to the World Depression." Bethell 4:57–82.

Tichi, Cecilia. *Shifting Gears: Technology, Literature, Culture in Modernist America.* Chapel Hill: U of North Carolina P, 1987.

Todorov, Tzvetan. *The Conquest of America.* Trans. Richard Howard. New York: Harper, 1984.

―――. *The Fantastic: A Structural Approach to a Literary Genre.* Trans. Richard Howard. Cleveland: P of Case Western Reserve U, 1973.

―――. *Grammaire du Décaméron.* The Hague: Mouton, 1969.

―――. "Macondo en Paris." *Texto crítico* 8 (1977): 36–45.

Toro, Alfonso de. "Estructura narrativa y temporal en *Cien años de soledad.*" *Revista iberoamericana* 128–29 (1984): 957–78.

Twentieth-Century European Authors 3. *Spanish: Márquez.* Prod. Christopher Stone. Presenter William Rowe. Reader Michael Bryant. Tape TLN10208K001. Programme HFA208K001. BBC. 18 April 1982. Salli Hornsby, Prod. Sec. 319 The Langham, PABX 5180/7684. London.

Valdés, Mario J. ed. *Inter-American Literary Relations: Proceedings of the Tenth Congress of the International Comparative Literature Association.* 27–30 August 1982. Vol. 3. New York: Garland, 1985.

Valencia Valderrama, M. "García Márquez et le cinema ou le cinema de García Márquez." Memoire. Paris: Université de Paris 3, Institut des Hautes Etudes de l'Amérique Latine. 1988.

Vargas Llosa, Mario. *García Márquez: Historia de un deicidio.* Barcelona: Barral, 1971.

―――. "Is Fiction the Art of Lying?" *New York Times Book Review* 7 Oct. 1984: 1, 40.

White, Hayden. "The Historical Text as Literary Artifact." *Tropics of Discourse.* Baltimore: Johns Hopkins UP, 1978. 81–100.

―――. *Metahistory.* Baltimore: Johns Hopkins UP, 1973.

Wiener, Philip D. *Dictionary of the History of Ideas: Studies of Selected Pivotal Ideas.* New York: Scribner's, 1973.

Williams, Raymond L. *Gabriel García Márquez.* Boston: Twayne, 1984.

Williams, William Carlos. *In the American Grain.* New York: New Directions, 1956.

Young, David, and Keith Hollaman. *Magical Realist Fiction: An Anthology.* New York: Longman, 1984.

Zamora, Lois Parkinson. "The Apocalyptic Vision in Contemporary American Fiction: Gabriel García Márquez, Thomas Pynchon, Julio Cortázar, and John Barth." *DAI* 38 (1978): 4808-A. U of California, Berkeley.

———. "The End of Innocence: Myth and Narrative Structure in Faulkner's *Absalom, Absalom!* and García Márquez's *Cien años de soledad.*" *Hispanic Journal* 4.1 (1982): 23–40.

———. "The Myth of Apocalypse and Human Temporality in García Márquez's *Cien años de soledad.*" *Symposium* 32.4 (1978): 341–55.

———. *Writing the Apocalypse: Historical Consciousness in Contemporary U.S. and Latin American Fiction.* Cambridge: Cambridge UP, 1989.

Zavala, Iris M. "*Cien años de soledad*: Crónica de Indias." *Insula* 25.286 (1970): 3, 11.

INDEX